Microsoft Dynamics GP 2013 Financial Management

Unleash the power of financial management
with tips, techniques, and solutions for
Microsoft Dynamics GP 2013

Ian Grieve

PUBLISHING

BIRMINGHAM - MUMBAI

Microsoft Dynamics GP 2013 Financial Management

First published: September 2013

Production Reference: 1300813

Published by Packt Publishing Ltd.
Livery Place
35 Livery Street
Birmingham B3 2PB, UK.

ISBN 978-1-78217-130-0

www.packtpub.com

Cover Image by Aniket Sawant (aniket_sawant_photography@hotmail.com)

Credits

Author
Ian Grieve

Reviewers
Mark Polino, CPA

Jivtesh Singh

Acquisition Editor
Akram Hussain

Commissioning Editor
Harsha Bharwani

Technical Editors
Vivek Pillai

Gaurav Thingalaya

Project Coordinator
Sherin Padayatty

Proofreader
Maria Gould

Indexer
Tejal R. Soni

Production Coordinator
Nitesh Thakur

Cover Work
Nitesh Thakur

About the Author

Ian Grieve is a Microsoft Dynamics GP and CRM certified consultant, specializing in the delivery of Microsoft Dynamics GP and CRM projects. He is a senior consultant at Perfect Image Ltd., a Microsoft Partner and VAR in the North East of England.

Ian has been working with Microsoft Dynamics GP since 2003. He has dealt with all aspects of the product life cycle from presales, to implementation, to technical and functional training, to post go-live support and subsequent upgrades, and process reviews.

Alongside his work with Microsoft Dynamics GP, in recent years he has fulfilled a similar role dealing with Microsoft Dynamics CRM, with special emphasis on project delivery and the training of end users on the management of sales, marketing, and services.

Ian is the co-author of *Microsoft Dynamics GP 2013 Cookbook*, produced *Microsoft Dynamics GP Techniques* online learning course, and was the technical reviewer for *Microsoft Dynamics CRM 2011 Applications (MB2-868) Certification Guide* and *Microsoft Dynamics CRM 2011 Cookbook*.

In his spare time, Ian runs the *azurecurve | Ramblings of a Dynamics GP Consultant* (http://www.azurecurve.co.uk/) blog dedicated to Microsoft Dynamics GP and related products and tries, often unsuccessfully, to squeeze in extra time for the Dynamics CRM related blog *coralcurve | A Consultant's Dabblings in Dynamics CRM* (http://www.coralcurve.co.uk/).

Acknowledgement

Thanks to my parents for their support through the years and my employer, Perfect Image, for being open to me taking on outside projects such as this book.

I also owe thanks to all of the clients I have worked with over the years, whose needs and questions have prompted me to learn ever more about Microsoft Dynamics GP, thereby putting me in a position to write this book.

Thanks to the Technical Reviewers, Mark Polino and Jivtesh Singh, for their valuable feedback which helped to make the book better.

Finally, thanks to the people at Packt Publishing, who I worked with through the course of the project.

About the Reviewers

Mark Polino, CPA is a principal consultant who has worked with Microsoft Dynamics GP for 15 years. He is the author or co-author of 4 books on Dynamics GP from Packt Publishing, and he created the successful *50 Tips in 50 Minutes for Dynamics GP* presentation series. Mark runs the premier Dynamics GP related website at www.dynamicaccounting.net.

Jivtesh Singh is a Microsoft Dynamics GP MVP, and a Microsoft Dynamics Certified Technology Specialist for Dynamics GP. Through his blog — which is widely read in the Dynamics GP community — he covers Dynamics GP tips, tricks, and news.

Jivtesh is a Dynamics GP Consultant and Systems Implementer, and has been associated with the Microsoft Technologies since the launch of Microsoft .NET Framework. Jivtesh has over 10 years of experience in the development and maintenance of enterprise software using coding best practices, refactoring and usage of design patterns, and test-driven development. Jivtesh recently built a Kinect interface to control the Microsoft Dynamics GP 2010 R2 Business Analyzer with gestures. Later, he built a part of the GP Future demo for Convergence GP Keynote.

Jivtesh has set up a custom search engine directory for the Dynamics GP blog at www.gpwindow.com to help with easier access of Dynamics GP resources for the GP community. With MVP Mark Polino, he has set up a Dynamics GP product directory, www.dynamicsgpproducts.com. He has also created a blog on Dynamics GP, www.jivtesh.com.

www.PacktPub.com

Support files, eBooks, discount offers and more

You might want to visit www.PacktPub.com for support files and downloads related to your book.

Did you know that Packt offers eBook versions of every book published, with PDF and ePub files available? You can upgrade to the eBook version at www.PacktPub.com and as a print book customer, you are entitled to a discount on the eBook copy. Get in touch with us at service@packtpub.com for more details.

At www.PacktPub.com, you can also read a collection of free technical articles, sign up for a range of free newsletters and receive exclusive discounts and offers on Packt books and eBooks.

http://PacktLib.PacktPub.com

Do you need instant solutions to your IT questions? PacktLib is Packt's online digital book library. Here, you can access, read and search across Packt's entire library of books.

Why Subscribe?

- Fully searchable across every book published by Packt
- Copy and paste, print and bookmark content
- On demand and accessible via web browser

Free Access for Packt account holders

If you have an account with Packt at www.PacktPub.com, you can use this to access PacktLib today and view nine entirely free books. Simply use your login credentials for immediate access.

Instant Updates on New Packt Books

Get notified! Find out when new books are published by following @PacktEnterprise on Twitter, or the Packt Enterprise Facebook page.

Table of Contents

Preface

Microsoft Dynamics GP is an Enterprise Resource Planning system from Microsoft. It is used throughout the world by organizations in many different sectors due to its renowned strengths in financial management. These strengths extend beyond the standard finance modules of the General Ledger, Fixed Asset Management, and the Accounts Payables and Receivables to include a number of modules, which add additional finance management capabilities to the core system.

These modules include Analytical Accounting (which allows for analysis of transactions below the account level), Cash Flow Management, and budgeting, as well as methods of controlling spending through purchase commitments or encumbering. This book introduces these modules and shows you how they can be used to improve financial management and reporting.

What this book covers

Chapter 1, Analytical Accounting, introduces the Analytical Accounting module and how to configure, use, and report on transactions compared to budget values.

Chapter 2, Cash Flow Management, covers using the setup of a cash flow forecast and how to use the Cash Flow Calendar and Cash Flow Explorer to track in-flows/out-flows of cash.

Chapter 3, Budget Creation and Maintenance, shows how budgets can be created, combined, and maintained in Microsoft Excel.

Chapter 4, Budget Reporting, looks at the methods for inquiring and reporting on budgets in Dynamics GP, including the use of Management Reporter 2012.

Chapter 5, Purchase Order Commitments, shows how Purchase Order Commitments can be used to control expenditure.

Chapter 6, Encumbrance Management, shows how encumbering transactions can be used to reduce over spending and keep funds available when payment becomes due.

What you need for this book

You will require the following software for this book:

- Microsoft Dynamics GP 2013 with the Fabrikam, Inc. sample company deployed
- Management Reporter 2012 RU6 with the Fabrikam, Inc. sample company imported
- SQL Server 2012 (or SQL Server 2008 R2)
- Microsoft Office 2013 (or Microsoft Office 2010)
- Windows Server 2012 (or Windows Server 2008 R2) with a Domain Controller available

Who this book is for

This book is for Dynamics GP users who are looking to improve their own financial management, or Microsoft Dynamics GP partners who are looking to improve the support of their clients. This book assumes that you have a basic understanding of business management systems and a working knowledge of the core Microsoft Dynamics GP financial and purchasing series.

Conventions

In this book, you will find a number of styles of text that distinguish between different kinds of information. Here are some examples of these styles, and an explanation of their meaning.

Code words in text are shown as follows: "Log on to Microsoft Dynamics GP using the sa or dynsa user accounts".

New terms and **important words** are shown in bold. Words that you see on the screen, in menus or dialog boxes for example, appear in the text like this: "Click on **OK** or **Save**, and close the **Posting Setup** window".

Reader feedback

Feedback from our readers is always welcome. Let us know what you think about this book—what you liked or may have disliked. Reader feedback is important for us to develop titles that you really get the most out of.

To send us general feedback, simply send an e-mail to feedback@packtpub.com, and mention the book title via the subject of your message.

If there is a topic that you have expertise in and you are interested in either writing or contributing to a book, see our author guide on www.packtpub.com/authors.

Customer support

Now that you are the proud owner of a Packt book, we have a number of things to help you to get the most from your purchase.

Errata

Although we have taken every care to ensure the accuracy of our content, mistakes do happen. If you find a mistake in one of our books—maybe a mistake in the text or the code—we would be grateful if you would report this to us. By doing so, you can save other readers from frustration and help us improve subsequent versions of this book. If you find any errata, please report them by visiting http://www.packtpub. com/submit-errata, selecting your book, clicking on the **errata submission form** link, and entering the details of your errata. Once your errata are verified, your submission will be accepted and the errata will be uploaded on our website, or added to any list of existing errata, under the Errata section of that title. Any existing errata can be viewed by selecting your title from http://www.packtpub.com/support.

Piracy

Piracy of copyright material on the Internet is an ongoing problem across all media. At Packt, we take the protection of our copyright and licenses very seriously. If you come across any illegal copies of our works, in any form, on the Internet, please provide us with the location address or website name immediately so that we can pursue a remedy.

Please contact us at copyright@packtpub.com with a link to the suspected pirated material.

We appreciate your help in protecting our authors, and our ability to bring you valuable content.

Questions

You can contact us at questions@packtpub.com if you are having a problem with any aspect of the book, and we will do our best to address it.

1
Analytical Accounting

Analytical Accounting is an add-on module to Microsoft Dynamics GP, which allows the extension of analysis of information beyond the segmental account. Without Analytical Accounting, additional reporting can only be accomplished by adding an additional segment to the chart of accounts. Analytical Accounting allows for this extended reporting without the need to change the chart of accounts, and also allows for the storage of information beyond monetary such as time (hours worked), space (size of room hired), or activity (such as marketing channel).

In this chapter we will take an introductory look at how to activate, configure, and enter transactions in Analytical Accounting. It is assumed that the Analytical Accounting feature has already been added to the installation of Microsoft Dynamics GP, and that GP Utilities has been run to update the databases.

Creating default records

Before Analytical Accounting can be used, there are several steps that must be completed. The first of them is to create the default records needed for Analytical Accounting.

To create the default records needed for Analytical Accounting, follow these steps:

1. Log on to Microsoft Dynamics GP using the sa or dynsa user accounts.

2. Open the **Analytical Accounting Setup Wizard** window in Dynamics GP by selecting **Administration** from the navigation pane on the left, and then clicking on **Setup** in the area page under **Setup | Company | Analytical Accounting**.

3. Make sure that the **Create Default Record** checkbox is marked, and then click on **Next**.

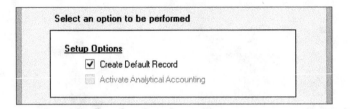

4. A listbox will be displayed showing the tasks, which will be processed. Click on **Finish** to proceed.

5. Once complete, click on **OK** to close the **Analytical Accounting Setup Wizard** window.

6. Repeat steps 1 to 5 for each company database.

This setup step needs to be performed in every company where Analytical Accounting is to be used as it creates all the records required for Analytical Accounting to function.

Setting up posting options

The final step needed before activating Analytical Accounting is to ensure that all posting options for **Create a Journal Entry Per** are set to either **Transaction**, as is most common, or to **Batch** with **Use Account Settings** marked.

To change the posting options, follow these steps:

1. Open the **Posting Setup** window in Dynamics GP by selecting **Administration** from the navigation pane on the left, and then clicking on **Posting** in the area page under **Setup | Posting**.

2. Check each **Series/Origin** combination, and ensure that **Use Account Settings** is marked, if the **Create a Journal Entry Per:** setting is set to **Batch**.

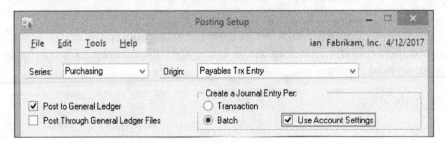

3. Click on **OK** or **Save,** once all **Series/Origin** combinations have been configured.

The Payroll module is slightly different to the other series in that there is an additional checkbox, **Post In Detail**, which must be marked for all origins except for **Period End Reports**. To enable this setting, follow these steps:

1. Open the **Posting Setup** window in Dynamics GP by selecting **Administration** from the navigation pane on the left, and then clicking on **Posting** in the area page under **Setup | Posting**.

2. Set **Series:** to **Payroll,** and **Origin:** to **All**.

3. Mark the **Post In Detail** checkbox (which is located above the **Use Account Settings** checkbox, when the **Series:** is set to **Payroll**).

4. Click on **OK** or **Save,** and close the **Posting Setup** window.

Activating Analytical Accounting

Now that the posting options have been configured as required by Analytical Accounting, the module can now be activated for use.

To activate Analytical Accounting, follow these steps:

1. Ensure there is a good backup of both the system (which is usually called Dynamics) and company database.

2. Log on to Microsoft Dynamics GP using the sa or dynsa user accounts.

3. Open the **Analytical Accounting Setup Wizard** window in Dynamics GP by selecting **Administration** from the navigation pane on the left, and then clicking on **Setup** in the area page under **Setup | Company | Analytical Accounting**.

4. Mark the **Activate Analytical Accounting** checkbox, and click on **Next**.

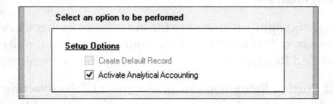

5. A listbox will be displayed showing the tasks that will be processed. Click on **Finish** to proceed.

6. Once complete, click on **OK** to close the **Analytical Accounting Setup Wizard**.

Assigning security roles and tasks

Now that Analytical Accounting has been activated, security needs to be configured, so that users without the **POWERUSER** role can use the functionality it offers. Analytical Accounting integrates into the standard Dynamics GP role-based security.

When installed, Analytical Accounting adds several default security roles and tasks. The default security tasks are:

ADMIN_AA_001*	CARD_AA_001*	RPT_AA_001*
ADMIN_AA_002*	INQ_AA_001*	TRX_AA_001*
AADEFAULTUSER*	INQ_AA_002*	

The default security roles are:

AA CLERK*	AA MANAGER*

Custom roles and tasks can be created if the default ones do not meet the needs of your organization. Once the required roles have been created, they need to be assigned to the users.

To assign the **AA MANAGER*** role to a user:

1. Open the **User Security Setup** window in Dynamics GP by selecting **Administration** from the navigation pane on the left, and then clicking on **User Security** in the area page under **Setup | System**.

2. Enter the **User:** to have the role assigned, and tab from the field.

3. In the **Roles:** scrolling window, mark the checkbox next to **AA MANAGER***.

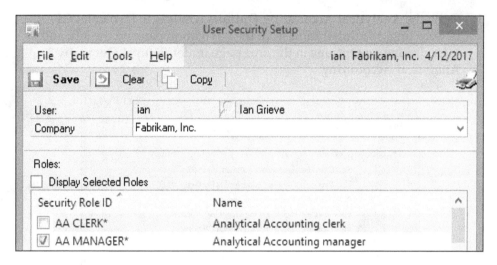

4. Click on **Save**.

The **AA CLERK*** role (or any custom role) can be assigned to the users in exactly the same way.

Analytical Accounting integrates with the standard Dynamics GP security model by creating the required operations, tasks, and roles. This means any user who currently understands the process of maintaining security will be able to grant access, or create the appropriate security to the users.

Configuring Analytical Accounting options

The next stage in configuring Analytical Accounting is to set up the options, which control the behavior of Analytical Accounting.

To amend the Analytical Accounting options:

1. Open the **Analytical Accounting Options** window in Dynamics GP by selecting **Administration** from the navigation pane on the left, and then clicking on **Options** in the area page under **Setup | Company | Analytical Accounting**.

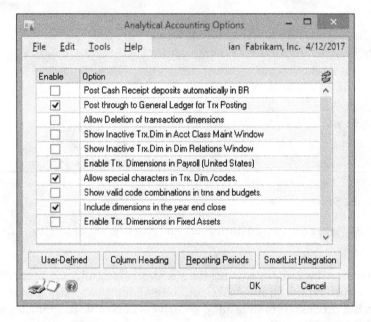

2. Mark the checkbox next to **Post through to General Ledger for Trx Posting** to allow transaction posting to post through the GL. A batch is automatically created and assigned to the transaction, during the transaction posting process.

3. Mark the **Include dimensions in the year end close** checkbox to transfer analytical data to history, during the year-end close process.

4. Click on the **User-Defined** button to change the field labels for the twenty user defined fields, which can be used for adding more information to the alphanumeric transaction dimensions.

5. Click on the **Column Heading** button to amend the column heading labels used on inquiries and reports.

6. Click on the **Reporting Periods** button to view the Fiscal and Calendar Views used in reports.

7. Click on the **SmartList Integration** button to select which SmartLists should be installed. To install a SmartList, mark the checkbox next to the **SmartList** folder in the scrolling window or, to install all, click on the **Mark All** button. Once all selections have been made, click on **Process**, then close the window.

8. Click on **OK** to close the **Analytical Accounting Options** window.

Configuring Assignment Setup

The **Assignment Setup** window allows for control over whether a module requires the full distribution amount to be assigned, or if a partial assignment can be posted. The exception to this is **Bank Reconciliation**, where you can post partial assignments, if the destination module of the posting allows partial assignments.

To amend the **Assignment Setup** window to allow partial assignment in the **General Ledger** module:

1. Open the **Assignment Options** window in Dynamics GP by selecting **Administration** from the navigation pane on the left, and then clicking on **Assignment** in the area page under **Setup | Company | Analytical Accounting**.

2. Unmark the checkbox in the **Full** column, next to the **General Ledger** module.

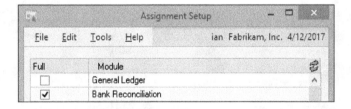

3. If you do not want to be warned about partial assignments when they have been allowed, mark the checkbox **No Warning when partial Assignments are Allowed** at the bottom of the window.

4. Click on **OK** to accept the setup.

By default, Analytical Accounting requires that the full distribution amount be assigned to an analysis code, but this is not always the way users want it to work. The **Assignment Setup** window grants users the flexibility to define if the distribution amount should be fully distributed, or if only a partial assignment is possible.

Creating transaction dimensions and dimension codes

Analysis information is entered via transaction dimensions. In this recipe we will take a look at the types of transaction dimensions that can be created.

There are four types of transaction dimensions that can be created: alphanumeric, numeric, yes/no, and date. An unlimited number of each type of transaction dimension can be created, with alphanumeric ones having codes created and attached.

To create an alphanumeric transaction dimension, perform the following steps:

1. Open the **Transaction Dimension Maintenance** window in Dynamics GP by selecting **Financial** from the navigation pane on the left, and then clicking on **Transaction Dimension** in the area page under **Cards | Financial | Analytical Accounting**.

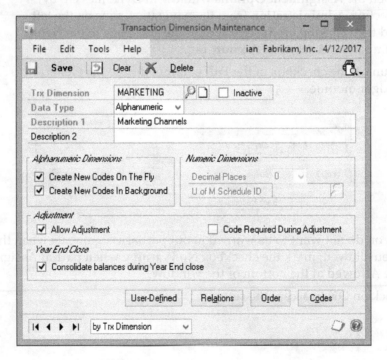

2. Enter MARKETING in the **Trx Dimension** field.

3. Enter Marketing Channels in **Description 1**.

4. Leave **Create New Codes On The Fly** checked to allow users to create new transaction dimension codes, when entering transactions.

5. Mark the **Consolidate balances during Year End close** checkbox to transfer analytical data to history during the year-end close.

6. Click on the **Codes** button in the bottom-right corner.

7. When prompted to save changes, click on **Save**.

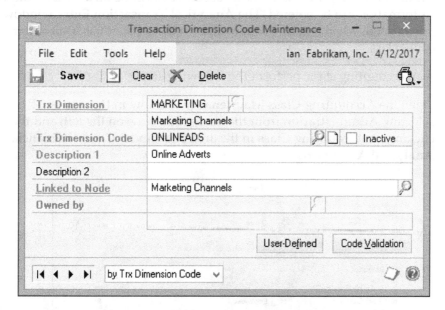

8. Enter ONLINEADS in the **Trx Dimension Code** field.

9. Enter Online Adverts in the **Description 1** field.

10. Click on the lookup button next to the **Linked to Node** field.

11. Ensure that Marketing Channels is selected, and click on **Select**.

12. Click on **Save**.

13. Repeat steps 7 to 11 to create transaction dimension codes for TWITTER, FACEBOOK, and GOOGLE+.

14. Click on **Save**, and close the **Transaction Dimension Code Maintenance** window.

15. Click on **Save**, and close the **Transaction Dimension Maintenance** window.

Only alphanumeric transaction dimensions can have transaction dimension codes created for them.

Only numeric transaction dimensions can have the number of decimal places, and a U of M Schedule ID can be specified.

Setting up an accounting class

An accounting class is a group of accounts used to determine for which accounts analysis information can be entered. The **Analytical Transaction Entry** window can only be opened, when entering transactions, if the account has been assigned to an account class.

To create an accounting class, perform the following steps:

1. Open the **Accounting Class Maintenance** window in Dynamics GP by selecting **Administration** from the navigation pane on the left, and then clicking on **Accounting Class** in the area page under **Cards | Financial | Analytical Accounting**.

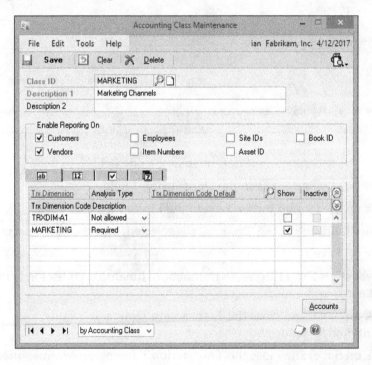

2. Enter MARKETING in the **Class ID** field.

3. Enter Marketing Channels in the **Description 1** field.

4. In the **Enable Reporting On** frame, mark the checkboxes next to **Customers** and **Vendors**, which will allow the customer number or vendor ID to be stored for reporting purposes, along with the transaction dimensions.

5. Change the **Analysis Type** of MARKETING to **Required**, and leave any other **Trx Dimension** column's **Analysis Type** as the default, **Not allowed**.

> The other types of **Analysis Type** available are **Fixed**, where a default **Trx Dimension Code value** must be selected, and cannot be changed during transaction entry; **Optional**, where a Trx Dimension Code can be selected, if desired; and **Not allowed**, which prevents the accounting class having access to the transaction dimension.

6. To assign accounts to the Accounting class, click on the **Accounts** button in the bottom-right corner of the window, and when prompted click on **Save** to save the Accounting class.

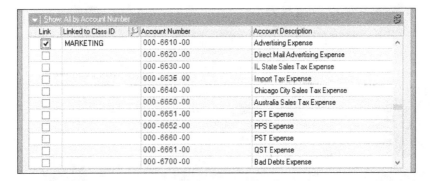

Link	Linked to Class ID	Account Number	Account Description
✓	MARKETING	000-6610-00	Advertising Expense
☐		000-6620-00	Direct Mail Advertising Expense
☐		000-6630-00	IL State Sales Tax Expense
☐		000-6635-00	Import Tax Expense
☐		000-6640-00	Chicago City Sales Tax Expense
☐		000-6650-00	Australia Sales Tax Expense
☐		000-6651-00	PST Expense
☐		000-6652-00	PPS Expense
☐		000-6660-00	PST Expense
☐		000-6661-00	QST Expense
☐		000-6700-00	Bad Debts Expense

7. Enter 000-6610-00 in the **Search by Account Number** field, and press *Tab*.

8. Mark the checkbox in the **Link** column next to 000-6610-00 to link it to the MARKETING accounting class.

9. Close the **Account Class Link** window.

10. Click on **Save**, and close the **Accounting Class Maintenance** window.

Analytical Accounting allows the creation of multiple accounting classes, which can each be allocated an unlimited number of accounts. However, any account can only be allocated to a single accounting class.

The accounting class defines which analysis codes are required, optional, or not allowed for the allocated accounts.

Granting user access to transaction dimensions

Now that transaction dimensions and accounting classes have been created, the final step needed before Analytical Accounting can be used for entering transactions and to grant user access to the transaction dimensions. Access can only be configured for alphanumeric transaction dimensions, whereas other transaction dimensions will be available to all users.

To grant user access, perform the following steps:

1. Open the **User Access to Trx Dimension Codes** window in Dynamics GP by selecting **Administration** from the navigation pane on the left, and then clicking on **User Access** in the area page under **Setup | Company | Analytical Accounting**.
2. Enter MARKETING in the **Trx Dimension** field.
3. Enter ONLINEADS in the **Trx Dimension Code** field.

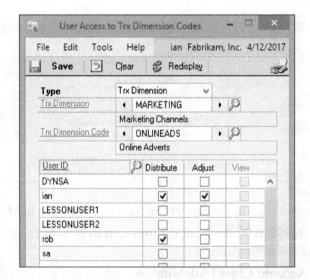

4. To give access to the dimensions during transaction entry, mark the checkbox in the **Dimension** column, next to the relevant users in the scrolling window.
5. To give access to the dimensions when making an adjustment to a posted transaction, mark the checkbox in the **Adjust** column next to the relevant users in the scrolling window.
6. Click on **Save**, and repeat steps 2 to 5 for all transaction dimension codes, which have been created.

Once granted access, users can enter or adjust transactions. Any new user created in Dynamics GP will need to have access granted before they can enter or adjust dimension information.

As discussed earlier, Analytical Accounting integrates with the standard security model of Dynamics GP. But, this is only to give access to the windows themselves. If a user is to be able to use the alphanumeric analysis codes, then the user needs to have access granted through **User Access to Trx Dimension Codes**.

When implementing the module, it would be worth speaking to your Dynamics GP partner for scripts to help automate the configuration of security for new codes.

Entering a transaction with Analytical Accounting information

With the setup of Analytical Accounting that we have covered so far in this recipe, we are now able to start entering transactions, and record the additional information via the transaction dimensions.

To enter a payable transaction with Analytical Accounting information, perform the following steps:

1. Open the **Purchase Order Entry** window in Dynamics GP by selecting **Purchasing** from the navigation pane on the left, and then clicking on **Purchase Order Entry** in the area page under **Transactions**.

2. Leave the **Type:** field as **Standard**, and tab through the **PO Number** field to have a purchase order number assigned.

3. Enter IMAGEMAK0001 in the **Vendor ID** field.

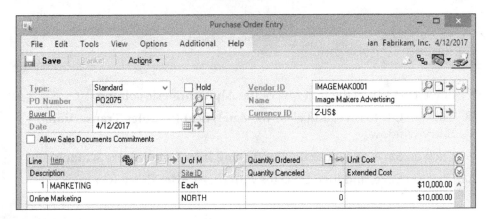

4. Enter MARKETING in the **Item** field.

5. Enter Each in the **U of M** field.

6. Enter 1 in **Quantity Ordered**.

7. Enter a unit cost of $10,000 in the **Unit Cost** field.

8. Enter Online Marketing in the **Description** field.

9. Enter NORTH in **Site ID**.

10. Click on the blue expansion arrow button next to the **Item** field header to open **Purchase Item Detail Entry**.

11. Click on the **Analytical Accounting** button next to the **Purchases Account** field to open the **Analytical Purchase Order Entry** window.

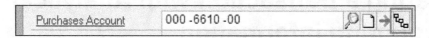

Purchases Account	000 -6610 -00	

12. Change the **Assign** % field to 66.67%.

13. Enter ONLINEADS in the **Alphanumeric** column of the scrolling window.

14. Enter Online adverts via adsense in the **Reference** field (this field is restricted to 30 characters).

15. Click on the **Assign** % column on the second row, and enter 33.33%.

16. Enter Sponsored tweets in the **Reference** field.

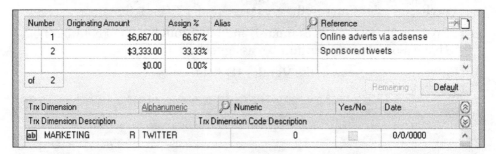

Number	Originating Amount	Assign %	Alias	Reference	
1	$6,667.00	66.67%		Online adverts via adsense	
2	$3,333.00	33.33%		Sponsored tweets	
	$0.00	0.00%			

of 2   Remaining   Default

Trx Dimension		Alphanumeric	Numeric		Yes/No	Date	
Trx Dimension Description			Trx Dimension Code Description				
ab MARKETING	R	TWITTER		0		0/0/0000	

17. Enter TWITTER in the first row of the **Alphanumeric** column.

18. Click on **OK** to save, and close the **Analytical Payables Transaction Entry** window.

19. Click on **Save**, and close the **Purchasing Item Detail Entry** window.

20. Click on **Save**, and then close the **Purchase Order Entry** window.

Analytical Accounting transaction dimension information can be broken down on each distribution line by changing the **Originating Amount** or **Assign** % values on the **Analytical Payables Transaction Entry** window, and then entering an **Originating Amount** or **Assign** % on the next line, in the scrolling window.

Microsoft Dynamics GP 2013 has seen several enhancements to the Analytical Accounting series such as integration to the Fixed Asset Management and the ability to duplicate analysis information when copying a transaction.

Duplicate analysis information when copying a transaction

Analysis information can be copied for three types of transactions: Purchase Orders, Sales Orders, and posted General Ledger transactions.

In each of the copy transaction windows, a new checkbox has been added. For example, in the **Copy Journal Entry** window, a new **Copy Analytical Accounting Information** checkbox has been added.

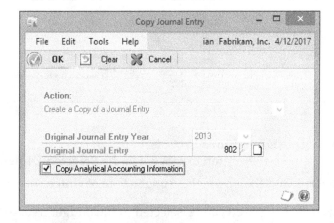

The same functionality has been added to the copy of Purchase and Sales Orders.

Integration of Analytical Accounting with Fixed Asset Management

In Dynamics GP 2013, Fixed Asset Management has been enhanced to allow the entry of analysis information for distribution accounts, which are linked to an account class. With the batch enhancements also added to Fixed Assets General Ledger Posting, the analysis information can be saved prior to posting the batch.

Creating an Analytical Accounting budget

Budgets can be created and tracked for reporting purposes to ensure expenditure is managed. There are several steps required to create budgets for analytical accounting dimensions.

The first step is to create a budget tree, which contains the selected dimensions. To create one, perform the following steps:

1. Open the **Budget Tree Maintenance** window in Dynamics GP by selecting **Financial** from the navigation pane on the left, and then clicking on **Budget Tree** in the area page under **Cards**.

2. Enter 2017 MARKETING in the **Budget Tree ID** field.

3. Enter 2017 Marketing Budget in the **Description** field.

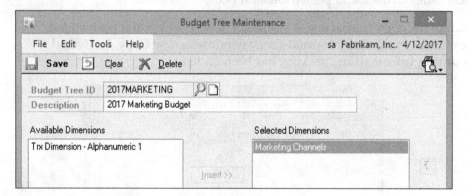

4. In the **Available Dimensions** list, select 2017 Marketing Budget, and click the **Insert>>** button to move it to the **Selected Dimensions** list.

5. Click on **Save**, and then close the **Budget Tree Maintenance** window.

As many dimensions as required can be selected in the budget tree, so that a budget value can be assigned, and dimensions can be included in more than one budget tree.

Once the budget tree has been created, the budget tree codes need to be assigned. To do this, perform the following steps:

1. Open the **Assign Budget Tree Codes** window in Dynamics GP by selecting **Financial** from the navigation pane on the left, and then clicking on **Assign Budget Tree Codes** in the area page under **Cards**.

2. Enter 2017 MARKETING in the **Budget Tree ID** field.

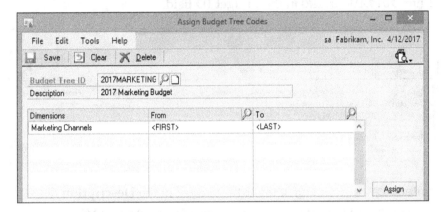

3. The **From** and **To** values will be set to <FIRST> and <LAST> respectively, but can be changed by either entering new values or performing a lookup.

   In this example, we'll assign budgets to all codes within the **Marketing Channels** dimension, so leave them as they are, and click on the **Assign** button.

   This will add the selected dimension codes to the **Dimension Code Tree** list in the lower-right corner of the window; codes can be removed or added using the controls to the left.

4. Click on the **Save** button, and then close the **Assign Budget Tree Codes** window.

With the budget tree set up and dimensions assigned, the budget amounts can now be entered. This is done in the **Analytical Accounting Budget Maintenance** window. To add budget amounts, perform the following steps:

1. Open the **Analytical Accounting Budget Maintenance** window in Dynamics GP by selecting **Financial** from the navigation pane on the left, and then clicking on **Assign Budget Tree Codes** in the area page under **Cards**.

2. Enter 2017MARKETING in the **Budget ID** field.

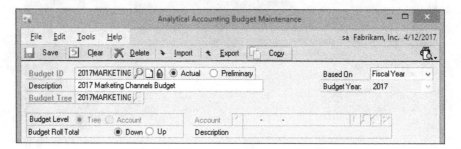

3. Enter 2017 Marketing Channels Budget in the **Description** field.

4. Leaved **Based On** set to **Fiscal Year**, and set the **Budget Year** field to 2017.

5. Set the **Budget Tree** field to 2017MARKETING.

6. Click on the **Methods** button near the lower-right of the window to open the **Budget Calculation Methods** window.

7. Set **Calculation Method** to **Yearly Budget Amount**.

8. Enter $48,000.00 in the **Amount** field.

9. Click on **Calculate** to close the **Budget Calculation Methods** window.

10. The $48,000.00 budget value will be evenly distributed in the **Node Budget Amounts** list.

11. Change the **Period4 4/1/2017** value to $2,000.00, and the **Period5 5/1/2017** value to $6,000.00.

12. The distributed $48,000.00 is at the top level of the budget, and needs to be rolled down to the dimension codes. To do this, click on the **Node** button to open the **Node Budget Roll Down** window.

13. **Calculate Method** can be set to either **Equal Split**, or left at the default of **Percentage**. Enter the following values:
    - ° 20.00% in **Facebook**
    - ° 10.00% in **Google+**
    - ° 40.00% in **Online Adverts**
    - ° 30.00% in **Twitter**

14. Click on the **Assign** button to accept the changes, and close the **Node Budget Roll Down** window.

15. Click on the **Save** button, and then close the **Analytical Accounting Budget Maintenance** window.

The budget that we have created is at dimension code level. Once a budget has been created and saved, it can be amended, and have more details applied to the budget by changing the **Budget Level** from **Tree** to **Account**. When this is done, each node in the **Dimension Code Tree** will need to have an account assigned.

If only a single account is required for a particular node, then this can be done by entering it in the **Account** field. If a range of nodes need to have the budget amount distributed, then open the **Account Budget Roll Down** window by clicking on the **Account** button.

Analytical Accounting budgets in Microsoft Excel

The **Analytical Accounting Budget Maintenance** window is used to create budgets within Microsoft Dynamics GP, but can also be used to export a budget to Microsoft Excel, and then import it again.

To export a budget to Microsoft Excel, follow these steps:

1. Open the **Analytical Accounting Budget Maintenance** window in Dynamics GP by selecting **Financial** from the navigation pane on the left, and then clicking on **Assign Budget Tree Codes** in the area page under **Cards**.

2. Perform a lookup, and select 2017MARKETING in the **Budget ID** field.

3. Click on the **Export** button on the toolbar.

4. Leave the **Excel Workbook** type set to **New workbook**. Before clicking on **OK**, make sure all windows are minimized as the Microsoft Excel **Save As** dialog will often open behind the main Dynamics GP window, and can be difficult to access.

5. Enter 2017MARKETING in the **File name**, and then click on **Open**.

Year-end processing

The **General Ledger Year-End Closing** window performs the bulk of actions required for the year-end processing of the Analytical Accounting module. When the year-end closing is performed, the following occurs:

1. All the previous years' analytical data for each account is transferred to the history (when history is being kept).

2. Analytical information for marked alphanumeric transaction dimensions for open year balance sheet accounts are brought forward as the beginning balances in the new fiscal year.

3. Analytical information for marked alphanumeric transaction dimensions for open year profit and loss accounts is consolidated and transferred to the Retained Earnings account.

   To ensure the analytical data is correct, balance brought forward transactions are created even if no profit and loss distributions exist for the year being closed and the profit and loss accounts' balances are zeroed.

4. Balances are brought forward for unit accounts.

5. The Analytical Accounting year-end closing report is printed.

Activating Analytical Accounting in an existing system

If you are activating Analytical Accounting in a Dynamics GP system which already had fiscal years closed, then you need to run the **Transfer Transaction Data to History** utility. This window is used to transfer analytical transaction information for closed years to the history and, in order to prevent duplicate brought forward balances, it is important that the transfer is completed before transactions are posted to a closed year or before closing an open year.

To transfer analysis information for closed years to history:

1. Open the **Transfer Transaction Data to History** window in Dynamics GP by selecting **Financial** from the navigation pane on the left, and then clicking on **Move Data To History** in the area page under **Utilities | Analytical Accounting**.

2. Select the action to perform:

   ° **Transfer transaction detail to history** will transfer all analysis information for the earliest closed year to the history.

   ° **Consolidate transactions and transfer detail to history** will consolidate transactions in the closed year based on the alphanumeric transaction dimensions marked for inclusion in the year-end close process. The analysis information will be moved to the history and closing balances brought forward to the next year.

   ° **Print transfer preview report only** allows you to print a report showing what the transfer will do.

3. After selecting one of the three options, click on the **OK** button.

Analytical Accounting inquiries

Analytical Accounting includes a number of inquiries, which can be used to view information.

Transaction Dimension Relation

The Transaction Dimension Relation is the simplest of the inquiry windows and does not have any user-definable criteria. The inquiry window shows the hierarchical structure, if any, created for the alphanumeric dimension codes.

Analytical Accounting – Journal Entry Inquiry

The Analytical Accounting – Journal Entry Inquiry can be used to view the analysis information for posted transactions as well as the consolidated analysis information for the balances that are brought forward.

To view a posted transaction's analysis information, perform the following steps:

1. Open the **Analytical Accounting – Journal Entry Inquiry** window in Dynamics GP by selecting **Financial** from the navigation pane on the left, and then clicking on **Journal Entry Inquiry** in the area page under **Inquiry | Analytical Accounting**.

2. In the **Budget ID** field, enter or perform a lookup for a posted transaction with analysis information. In this example, I am using journal 3,454.

3. Use the navigation buttons next to the **Distribution** field to scroll through the distributions to view the analysis information in the window at the bottom of the window.

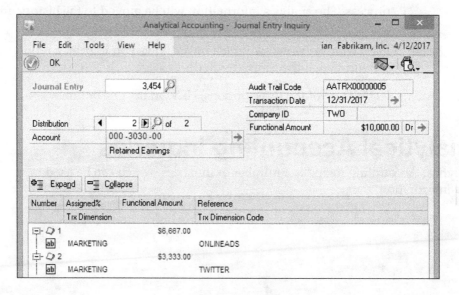

Distribution Query Wizard

The Analytical Accounting Distribution Query Wizard is used to create, execute, and export queries to a Microsoft Excel worksheet and allows queries to be saved for later reuse.

Posted analysis information for transaction dimension codes that have subsequently been set to inactive status can be viewed, as well as the consolidated balances that are brought forward when a fiscal year is closed; the beginning value of the period range must be 0 in the **Distribution Query Wizard – Finish** window in order to view consolidated balances.

To use the Distribution Query Wizard to run a query, follow these steps:

1. Open the **Distribution Query Wizard** window in Dynamics GP by selecting **Financial** from the navigation pane on the left, and then clicking on **Distribution Query Wizard** in the area page under **Inquiry | Analytical Accounting**.
2. Select **Execute Ad Hoc Query**, and click on **Next**.
3. On the **Column Selection** step, select the following items in the **Available Columns** list, and then click on the **Insert>>** button after selecting each one:
    ○   **Journal Entry**
    ○   **GL Posting Date**
    ○   **Account Number**
    ○   **Account Description**
    ○   **Credit Amount**
    ○   **Debit Amount**
    ○   **Vendor ID**
    ○   **Item Number**
    ○   **Trx Dimension – Alphanumeric**
    ○   **Marketing Channels**
4. Click on **Next**.
5. In the list, select **Marketing Channels** to populate the **Selected Column** field.
6. Set the **Select Type** to **Is Between**.

7. Set the range to FACEBOOK and TWITTER.

8. Mark the **Balance Sheet** checkbox.

9. Click on **Next**.

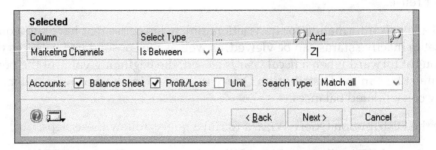

10. Click on **Next**.

11. Click on **Next** to proceed without **Order By Selection**.

12. On the **Completing the Options** step, set **Period** in the **From** field to 1 and the **To** field to 12.

13. Enter 2017 Marketing Channels in the **Comment** field.

14. Click on **Finish** to generate the inquiry to Excel.

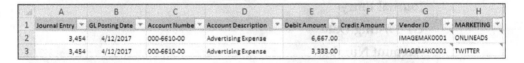

The preceding steps show how to create an ad hoc query, but the inquiry also allows queries to be saved for later by adding a couple of extra steps to them. To save a query, perform these steps:

1. Open the **Distribution Query Wizard** window in Dynamics GP by selecting **Financial** from the navigation pane on the left, and then clicking on **Distribution Query Wizard** in the area page under **Inquiry | Analytical Accounting**.

2. Select **Query Maintenance** and click on **Next**.

3. In the **Query ID** field, enter 2017MARKETING.

4. Enter 2017 Marketing Channels in the **Description** field.

5. Click on **Next**.

6. Use the steps from the Ad Hoc Query steps mentioned previously to create the query and save it for use.

The query can be run using the third option on **Distribution Query Wizard**. To do so, follow these steps:

1. Open the **Distribution Query Wizard** window in Dynamics GP by selecting **Financial** from the navigation pane on the left, and then clicking on **Distribution Query Wizard** in the area page under **Inquiry | Analytical Accounting**.

2. Select **Execute Existing Query**, and click on **Next**.

3. Select **2017MARKETING** in **Query ID**, and click on **Next**.

4. Enter a **Comment** and click on **Finish** to run the query as saved, or use the **<** **Back** button to amend the query.

There is no limit to the number of queries that can be saved in this inquiry.

Multilevel Query Wizard

The Analytical Accounting Multilevel Query Wizard is used to create, execute, and export queries to a Microsoft Excel worksheet. Queries can be created to analyze the data based on transaction dimensions, which can include dimensions set to inactive as well as consolidated balances that are brought forward when a fiscal year is closed.

As with the Distribution Query Wizard, queries can be saved for reuse as well as being constructed and used on an ad hoc basis.

Creating and saving a Multilevel Query is the same as creating and saving a Distribution Query. In this example, we'll cover creating an ad hoc query. To create one, perform the following steps:

1. Open the **Multilevel Query Wizard** window in Dynamics GP by selecting **Financial** from the navigation pane on the left, and then clicking on **Multilevel Query Wizard** in the area page under **Inquiry | Analytical Accounting**.

2. Select **Execute Ad Hoc Query**, and click on **Next**.

3. On the **Level Selection** step, select the following items in the **Available Items** list, and click on the **Insert>>** button after selecting each one:

    ◦ **Time**

    ◦ **Account Number**

    ◦ **Marketing Channels**

4. Click on **Next**.

5. On the **Column Spreads** step, click on **Next**.

6. Enter MT_ACCOUNT, or perform a lookup and select MT_ACCOUNT as the **Tree** for the **Account Number** level.

7. Enter MT_MARKETING, or perform a lookup and select MT_MARKETING as the **Tree** for the Marketing Channels level.

8. Click on **Next**.

9. Mark the **Balance Sheet** checkbox, and click on **Next**.

10. On the **Column Selection** step, select the following **Available Columns** and click on the **Insert>>** button.

    ° **Net change**

    ° **Net change YTD**

11. Click on **Next**.

12. Set the **Period** range in the **From** field to 4 and the **To** field to 4.

13. Click on **Finish** to generate the query.

14. In the resulting Excel spreadsheet, click on the expansion button to show the multilevel data.

	A	B	C	D	E
1	2017MARKETING 2017 Marketing Channels			Net change	Net change YTD
2	Period 4/2017			10,000.00	10,000.00
3		000-6610-00 (Advertising Expense)		10,000.00	10,000.00
4			ONLINEADS (Online Adverts)	6,667.00	6,667.00
5			TWITTER (Twitter)	3,333.00	3,333.00
6	Total Query			10,000.00	10,000.00

Analytical Accounting Budget vs Actual Inquiry

The **Analytical Accounting Budget vs Actual Inquiry** window can be used to view the actual and budgeted amounts for a selected node along with the variance calculated as both an amount and a percentage. To use the inquiry, perform the following steps:

1. Open the **Analytical Accounting Budget vs Actual Inquiry** window in Dynamics GP by selecting **Financial** from the navigation pane on the left, and then clicking on **Budget vs Actual** in the area page under **Inquiry | Analytical Accounting**.

2. Enter 2017MARKETING in the **Budget ID** field.

3. Enter 2017 in the **Year** field.

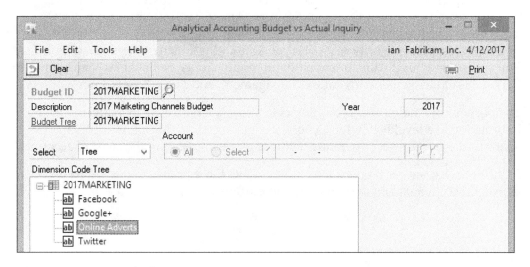

4. In the **Dimension Code Tree** list, click on **Online Adverts** to populate the grid at the bottom of the window with the actual and budget values for the selected dimension code.

Analytical Account SmartLists

If deployed, there are a number of SmartLists available to inquire upon the Analytical Accounting data, which work in the same fashion as standard SmartLists.

The SmartLists can be broken down into two types: Setup and Transaction, with the former having a larger number of SmartLists.

Setup	Transaction
AA Accounting Classes	AA Dimension Balances
AA Distribution Queries	AA Transactions
AA Multilevel Queries	
AA Trees	
AA Trx Dimension Codes	
AA Trx Dimensions	

Summary

In this chapter we have taken an introductory look at the Analytical Accounting module covering setup and transaction entry. Analytical Accounting is not a stand-alone module, but one which operates by adding additional functionality into other modules. The majority of Analytical Accounting functionality lives within the Financial series, but it adds functionality to modules such as Payables Management, Receivables Management, Inventory Management, and Fixed Assets among others.

The purpose of Analytical Accounting is to allow the recording of analysis information at a level below the General Ledger account. This allows deeper analysis of expenditure, or revenue, without overcomplicating the chart of accounts.

In the next chapter, we'll take a look at how Cash Flow Management can be used to oversee the management of inflows and outflows of cash.

2
Cash Flow Management

Cash Flow Management can be used to keep a track of cash flow within Microsoft Dynamics GP and also to forecast cash flow based on one or more checkbook balances with or without work/adjustment transactions such as deposits, payments, or reconciliation adjustments that are not part of the checkbook balances.

Cash Flow Management can be used to complete the following tasks:

- Create an unlimited number of different cash flow forecasts
- Create scenarios without recording transactions
- Summarize daily inflows and outflows of cash in the Cash Flow Calendar
- View the summary of any given day's cash inflow and outflow
- Run summary or detailed reports on weekly and monthly cash flow

Cash Flow Management is installed automatically with Microsoft Dynamics GP and is licensed as a part of the starter pack, and so is available to all users.

Creating a cash flow forecast

Microsoft Dynamics GP Cash Flow Management supports the creation of unlimited cash flow forecasts, one of which can be defined as the default.

To create a default cash flow forecast which includes transactions against all checkbooks from all series, perform the following steps:

1. Open the **Cash Flow Forecast** window in Dynamics GP by selecting **Financial** from the Navigation Pane on the left, and then clicking on **Cash Flow Forecast** in the area page under **Setup** | **Financial**.

2. Enter DEFAULT in the **Forecast ID** field.

3. Mark the **Default** checkbox.

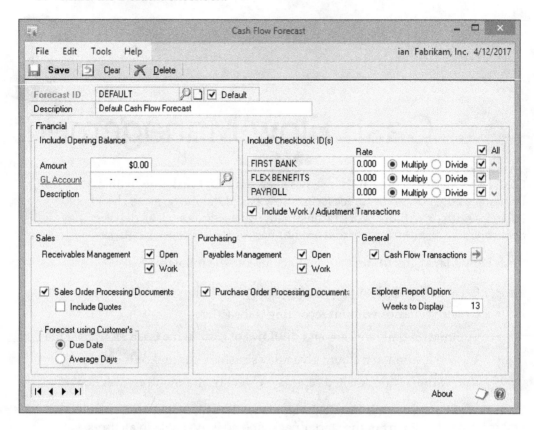

4. Enter Default Cash Flow Forecast in the **Description** field.

5. Mark the **All** checkbox in the **Include Checkbook ID(s)** frame.

6. Mark the **Open** and **Work** checkboxes for **Receivables Management**.

7. Mark the **Sales Order Processing Documents** checkbox.

8. Mark the **Open** and **Work** checkboxes for **Payables Management**.

9. Mark the **Purchase Order Processing Documents** checkbox.

10. To include "what if?" transactions mark the **Cash Flow Transactions** checkbox.

11. Enter 13 in the **Weeks to Display** field.

12. Click on **Save**, and close the **Cash Flow Forecast** window.

Now that a default cash flow forecast has been created, we can progress on to using the Cash Flow Management module.

Cash flow forecasts are how the cash inflows and outflows are tracked within Dynamics GP. Each cash flow forecast created can have different bank accounts and options such as the opening balance, defined to allow different forecasts to be used.

Using the Cash Flow Calendar

The Cash Flow Calendar displays the inflow and outflow of cash according to the rules defined against the default cash flow forecast.

To view the Cash Flow Calendar, perform the following steps:

1. Open the **Cash Flow Calendar** window in Dynamics GP by selecting **Financial** from the Navigation Pane on the left, and then clicking on **Cash Flow Calendar** in the area page under **Inquiry | Financial**.

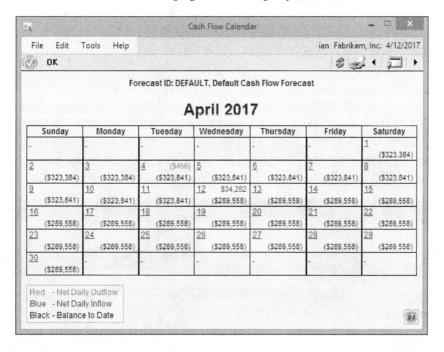

2. As the legend shows, a red entry wrapped in parentheses on the first line of a date shows a net daily outflow of cash, as occurred on the 4th of April; and a blue entry shows a net daily inflow of cash as shown on the 12th of April. The balance in black on the second line shows the balance to date.

3. Double-clicking on a calendar cell will launch the **Cash Flow Explorer** window, where the details of the movement can be seen.

4. When the **Cash Flow Calendar** window is opened from the menu or area page, only the default cash flow forecast can be viewed. The **Cash Flow Explorer** window can be used to access Cash Flow Calendars of other forecasts.

5. The Cash Flow Calendar provides the ability to print a cash flow monthly report.

6. The cash flow monthly report is printed by clicking on the **Print** button and selecting the destination of the report.

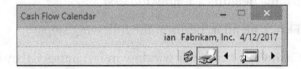

The **Cash Flow Explorer** window can be used to view the details of the movement on each date. When the window is first opened, it will show the transactions for the default cash flow forecast for the user date, but this can be changed to view the details of other cash flow forecasts.

To use the Cash Flow Explorer, perform the following steps:

1. Open the **Cash Flow Explorer** window in Dynamics GP by selecting **Financial** from the Navigation Pane on the left, and then clicking on **Cash Flow Explorer** in the area page under **Inquiry | Financial**.

2. The details of the cash flow can now be seen; click on **4** in the **Tuesday** column to launch the **Cash Flow Explorer** window for the 4th of April.

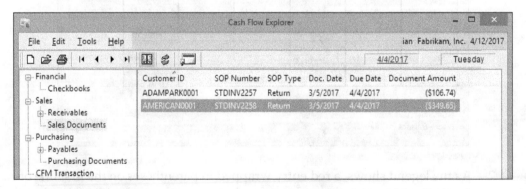

3. Expand the **Sales** node, and click on **Sales Documents** to see the two transactions, which comprise the net daily outflow for 4th April.

4. Double-click on **STDINV2258** to open the **Sales Transaction Inquiry Zoom** window to see details of the transaction.

5. Close the **Sales Transaction Inquiry Zoom** window.

6. Close the **Cash Flow Calendar** window.

Cash Flow Explorer provides an easy-to-use interface which allows the user to browse through dates and see which modules have transactions, and then drill down to see details of the transactions.

When opened, the **Cash Flow Explorer** window shows the default cash flow forecast, which we have created at the start of this chapter. Cash Flow Management can have an unlimited number of cash flow forecasts created in it, and Cash Flow Explorer can be used to inquire upon these as well.

It can also be used to launch the **Cash Flow Calendar** window for any cash flow forecast and also to produce weekly cash flow reports.

Viewing other cash flow forecasts

To use Cash Flow Explorer to view forecasts other than the default, perform the following steps:

1. Open the **Cash Flow Explorer** window in Dynamics GP by selecting **Financial** from the Navigation Pane on the left, and then clicking on **Cash Flow Explorer** in the area page under **Inquiry | Financial**.

2. Click on the Open button as shown in the following screenshot:

3. The **Forecasts** window will open showing all cash flow forecasts that have been created; select the desired forecast.

4. Click on **Select** to close the window.

The **Cash Flow Explorer** window will now display the selected cash flow forecast; the **Forecast ID** and **Description** fields will be displayed in the windows status bar.

Launching Cash Flow Calendar from Cash Flow Explorer

As well as being launched from the area page, the **Cash Flow Calendar** inquiry window can also be loaded from the **Cash Flow Explorer** window by performing the following steps:

1. Open the **Cash Flow Explorer** window in Dynamics GP by selecting **Financial** from the Navigation Pane on the left, and then clicking on **Cash Flow Explorer** in the area page under **Inquiry | Financial**.

2. Click on the Calendar button as highlighted in the following screenshot:

Once launched from **Cash Flow Explorer**, the Cash Flow Calendar can be used to browse the selected cash flow forecast.

Printing weekly cash flow reports

There are three reports available from **Cash Flow Explorer**: **Weekly Summary**, **Weekly Summary by Source**, and **Weekly Detail by Source**. These reports are printed by clicking on the print icon and selecting the relevant option.

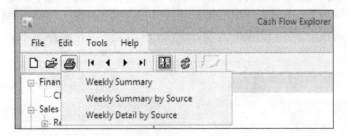

"What if?" transactions

Cash Flow Management is mainly used to track the inflow and outflow of cash in Microsoft Dynamics GP by using cash flow forecasts. As with any good forecast module, "what if?" transactions can be entered to either include transactions which are due but have not yet arrived, or to model the predicted impact of future business operations.

To use a "what if?" transaction, perform the following steps:

1. Open the **Cash Flow Transactions** window in Dynamics GP by selecting **Financial** from the Navigation Pane on the left, and then clicking on **Cash Flow Transaction** in the area page under **Setup | Financial**.

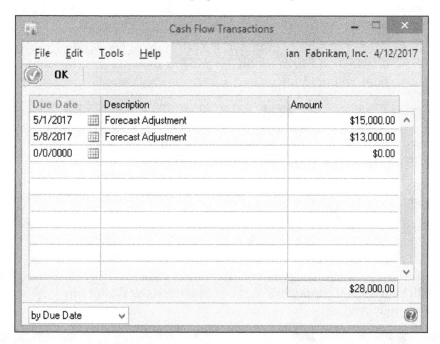

2. Enter 5/1/2017 in the **Due Date** field.
3. Enter Forecast Adjustment in the **Description** field.
4. Enter $15,000.00 in the **Amount** field.
5. Repeat steps 2 to 5 to enter a transaction of $13,000.00 for 8/5/2017.

An unlimited number of cash flow transactions can be entered and removed when they are no longer required. These transactions will only be included in the cash flow forecast if the **Cash Flow Transactions** checkbox on the forecast has been checked.

"What if?" transactions appear in the cash flow forecast and Cash Flow Calendar, affecting the figures. They're used to predict the impact of expected future transactions without having an impact on the general ledger balances.

Once the cash flow transaction has been entered, it will be included in the **Cash Flow Calendar** and **Cash Flow Explorer** windows. To view the transactions, perform the following steps:

1. Open the **Cash Flow Calendar** window in Dynamics GP by selecting **Financial** from the Navigation Pane on the left, and then clicking on **Cash Flow Calendar** in the area page under **Inquiry | Financial**.

2. Click on the Next Month button in the top-right of the window to change the calendar to May; the cells for the 1st and 8th show the $15,000 and $13,000 transactions entered previously.

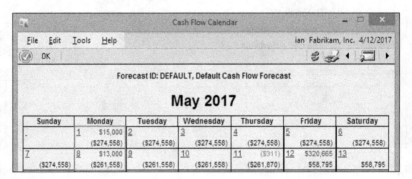

3. Click on the cell containing $15,000 to launch the **Cash Flow Explorer** window.

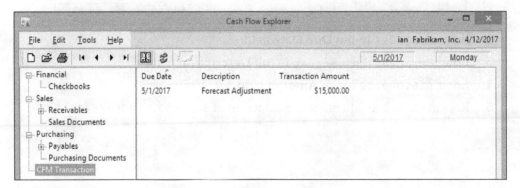

4. Click on **CFM Transaction** to view the "what if?" transactions.

5. Close the **Cash Flow Explorer** window.

6. Close the **Cash Flow Calendar** window.

Cash flow transactions can be removed once they are no longer required for the forecast.

Summary

In this chapter we looked at Cash Flow Management, how to create and view forecasts, and how to enter "what if?" transactions to explore scenarios. The next chapter will cover the creation and maintenance of budgets in Dynamics GP 2013.

3
Budget Creation and Maintenance

One of the most important accounting tools for a business is the budget, which is generally created on an annual basis to outline the expected needs of each department or business area.

A major benefit of budgets is the ability to control spending on certain operations by restricting the funds available for spending, which can require managers and buyers to find new vendors or suppliers to meet budget limits.

Budgets also allow companies to plan for future growth and expansion, and allow the creation of a financial roadmap.

Dynamics GP provides a flexible and easy-to-use budget creation and maintenance utility, which allows for comparison to the previous year's actual and budget figures during the budget creation process.

Creating a budget with Microsoft Excel

Budgets can be created in Dynamics GP directly, but the most efficient way of creating a budget for use in Microsoft Dynamics GP is to create it using Microsoft Excel.

There are four steps to create a budget in Dynamics GP. They are as follows:

1. Create the budget.
2. Export the budget to Microsoft Excel from Dynamics GP.
3. Edit the budget in Microsoft Excel.
4. Import the budget back into Dynamics GP.

It is strongly recommended that the budget be created in Dynamics GP and exported to Microsoft Excel for editing, as the import process requires the structure of the file to be exactly the same as the one being exported. The attempts to create the budget template manually can be very problematic.

To create a budget in Microsoft Excel, follow the given steps:

1. Open the **Budget Selection** window in Dynamics GP by clicking on **Financial** from the Navigation Pane on the left, and then clicking on **Budgets** in the area page under **Cards | Financial**.

2. Click on the **New** button and then navigate to **using Budget Wizard for Excel**.

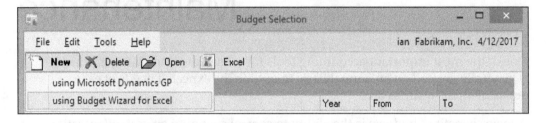

3. On the **Welcome to the Budget Wizard for the Excel** window, click on **Next**.

4. Many of the organizations I have dealt with have used multiple budgets throughout the year. For example, they'll create an initial budget, a half-year forecast, and a master budget for reporting. As such, I always recommend that the year be placed at the start of the **Budget ID**, to group them together in the list of budgets. Following this recommendation, enter 2017 MASTER in the **Enter an ID for this budget** field.

5. Enter Master Budget for 2017 in **Enter a description for this budget**.

6. Leave **Select how to base this budget** set to Fiscal Year and change **Select the date range for this budget** to 2017.

7. Click on **Next** to progress to the next step.

8. Budgets can be based on one of the four calculation methods. In this example, click on **Other Budget Percent**.

Select a budget calculation method which will be used to create default budget amounts in Excel.

> Open Year Percent
> Other Budget Percent
> Historical Year Percent
> Blank Budget

Other Budget Percent
Calculates amounts from another budget by increasing or decreasing by a set percentage for the new budget.

9. Click on **Next**.

10. Set the **Select a source budget ID** field to BUDGET 2008.

11. Set **Increase by** to 2.50% and click on **Next**.

12. If a worksheet for actual figures is to be output to the Excel budget, check the relevant checkbox, otherwise click on **Next**.

13. The Account Verification step allows the selected accounts to be reviewed and unwanted ones to be removed. In this case, click on **Next** to proceed.

14. Accept **A new workbook** as the Excel workbook to use, and click on **Next**.

15. Before clicking on **Finish** to complete the budget creation, minimize all open windows other than the **Budget Wizard for Excel** window to prevent the **Excel Save As** dialog popping behind a window, and being inaccessible. Once the windows have been minimized, click on **Finish**.

16. Click on **Save** to save the 2017 MASTER.xlsx file to your **Documents** folder.

Editing a budget in Microsoft Excel

Now that the 2017 MASTER budget has been created in Microsoft Excel by copying the MASTER 2008 budget, and adding 2.5 percent, the budget can be edited in Excel before being imported into Dynamics GP.

It is very important that the column structure and the header rows of the spreadsheet are not altered; if they are, the budget will not import back into Dynamics GP.

To edit the budget, perform the following steps:

1. Open the `2017 MASTER.xlsx` spreadsheet you saved to your **Documents** folder.

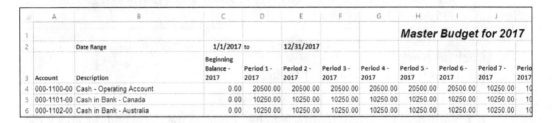

	A	B	C	D	E	F	G	H	I	J	
1									**Master Budget for 2017**		
2		Date Range	1/1/2017	to	12/31/2017						
3	Account	Description	Beginning Balance - 2017	Period 1 - 2017	Period 2 - 2017	Period 3 - 2017	Period 4 - 2017	Period 5 - 2017	Period 6 - 2017	Period 7 - 2017	Perio 2017
4	000-1100-00	Cash - Operating Account	0.00	20500.00	20500.00	20500.00	20500.00	20500.00	20500.00	10250.00	10
5	000-1101-00	Cash in Bank - Canada	0.00	10250.00	10250.00	10250.00	10250.00	10250.00	10250.00	10250.00	10
6	000-1102-00	Cash in Bank - Australia	0.00	10250.00	10250.00	10250.00	10250.00	10250.00	10250.00	10250.00	10

2. Change the cells **D5**, **E5**, **F5**, **G5**, **H5**, and **I5** to `20500.00`.

3. Click on the **Save** button and close Microsoft Excel (a common mistake is not to close Microsoft Excel which then causes the import to fail due to a file lock).

As many changes as required can be made to the Excel spreadsheet, and additional account codes can be inserted if required. The changes are only within the Excel spreadsheet; to apply the changes, the spreadsheet needs to be imported into Dynamics GP.

Importing a budget from Microsoft Excel

Now that the 2017 MASTER budget has been edited in Microsoft Excel, we now need to import it back to Dynamics GP.

To import the budget into Dynamics GP, perform the following steps:

1. Open the **Budget Selection** window in Dynamics GP by clicking on **Financial** from the Navigation Pane on the left, and clicking on **Budgets** in the area page under **Cards | Financial**.

2. Click on the **Excel** button and then click on **Import from Excel** which will launch **Budget Wizard from Excel**.

3. On the **Welcome** page, click on **Next**.

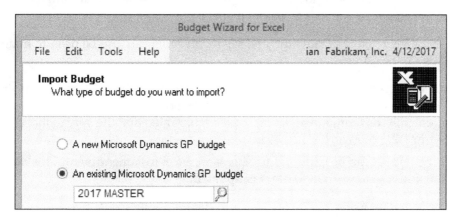

4. Click on **An Existing Microsoft Dynamics GP budget** and enter 2017 MASTER.

5. Click on **Next**.

6. Click on **Browse...** and then click on the Excel spreadsheet 2017 MASTER. xlsx from your **Documents** folder.

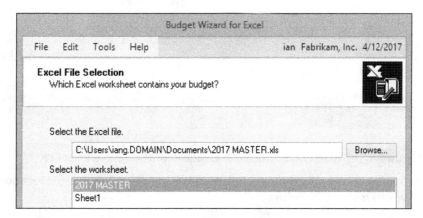

7. Click on the **2017 MASTER** worksheet and click on **Next**.

8. Click on **Finish** to complete the import.

Maintaining budgets

After a budget is created it tends to be dynamic, as business and budgeting needs change during the course of the year, resulting in budget values changing or needing to be moved from one account to another.

As well as being used to create budgets, Microsoft Excel can also be used to maintain them. This can be done in one of two ways.

- The **Open** button can be clicked and this will open the existing Microsoft Excel spreadsheet, which has previously been exported. This method is not generally recommended, as there is no guarantee that the spreadsheet on your PC or network share is the most up-to-date.

- The budget can be exported to Microsoft Excel for amendment. This method ensures the up-to-date budget is updated.

To amend a budget using Microsoft, perform the following steps:

1. Open the **Budget Selection** window in Dynamics GP by clicking on **Financial** from the Navigation Pane on the left, and clicking on **Budgets** in the area page under **Cards | Financial**.

2. Click on the **2017 MASTER** budget and click on the **Excel** button. Then, click on **Export to Excel** which will launch the **Budget Wizard from Excel**.

3. Click on **New workbook** for **Excel Workbook type**.

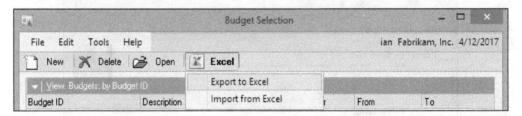

4. Minimize the main Dynamics GP window and then click on **OK**.

5. In the **Excel Save As** dialog, click on **Save** to accept the default location of your **Documents** folder.

Once the export is finished, the spreadsheet can be updated and then imported back into Dynamics GP as we covered previously.

If only minor amendments are required to a budget, then using Microsoft Excel can be likened to using the proverbial sledgehammer to crack the equally proverbial walnut.

Microsoft Dynamics GP provides an alternative method for editing and creating budgets, which is far quicker than using Excel when a small number of changes are required.

To edit a budget through Microsoft Dynamics GP, perform the following steps:

1. Open the **Budget Selection** window in Dynamics GP by clicking on **Financial** from the Navigation Pane on the left, and clicking on **Budgets** in the area page under **Cards | Financial**.

2. Click on the **2017 MASTER** budget.

3. Click on the **Open** button and then click on **using Microsoft Dynamics GP** to open the **Budget Maintenance** window.

4. Enter 000-1100-00 in the **Account** field.

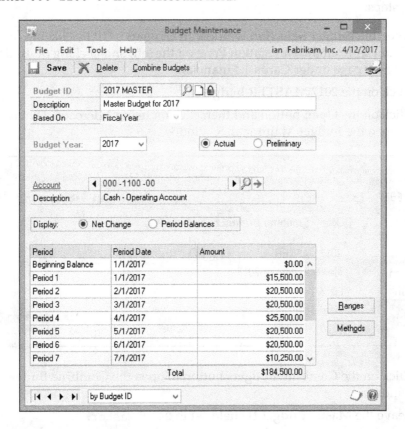

5. Decrease the **Amount** for **Period 1** to $15,500.00.

6. Increase the **Amount** for **Period 4** to $25,500.00.

7. Click on **Save** and close the **Budget Maintenance** window.

Combining budgets

Until Microsoft Dynamics GP 2010, one of the features most commonly asked about by customers was missing. This was the ability to combine budgets together so that separate budgets could be created for each budget holder, and then merged together in Dynamics GP rather than in Microsoft Excel.

Two budgets are required for the combine function. We can use the 2017 MASTER budget as the one into which we will merge a second budget, but we will need to create this second budget first. This can be done using the steps already covered on creating a new budget and create a budget for the sales division (Division Segment = 300) called **2017 SALES**.

To combine the 2017 SALES budget with the 2017 MASTER budget, perform the following steps:

1. Open the **Budget Selection** window in Dynamics GP by clicking on **Financial** from the Navigation Pane on the left, and clicking on **Budgets** in the area page under **Cards | Financial**.

2. Click on the **2017 MASTER** budget.

3. Click on the **Open** button and then click on **using Microsoft Dynamics GP** to open the **Budget Maintenance** window.

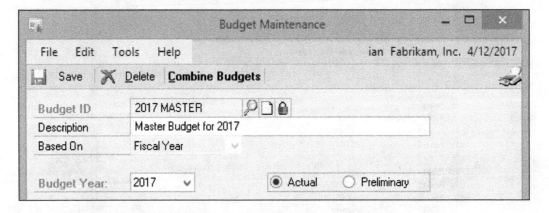

4. Click on the **Combine Budgets** button to open the **Combine Budgets** window.

5. Leave the **Master Budget ID** field set to 2017 Master.

6. Enter 2017 SALES in the **Combine with Budget ID** field.

7. Click on **Process** to enact the combine of 2017 SALES into 2017 MASTER.

8. Click on **OK** to confirm the **Process was successful** message box.

One important point to remember is that the combine budgets feature merges the budgets together. It does not overwrite the destination budget values with those from the one being merged in. Combine should be used only when a value has not been entered or the budget of the destination is to be increased (or decreased) by the amount on the budget being merged in.

Entering budget transactions

Another feature introduced in Microsoft Dynamics GP 2010 is the ability to enter budget transactions to adjust the budgets previously created. The advantage of using budget transactions over updating the budget via **Budget Maintenance** or Excel is that a record can be maintained of what adjustments to the budget have been made.

There are two settings that can be reviewed before starting to use budget transactions. The first is the **Budget Journal Entry** number, which can be increased from the default of 1, and the other is the **Maintain History** checkbox for **Budget Transactions**.

To maintain these settings, perform the following steps:

1. Open the **General Ledger Settings** window in Dynamics GP by clicking on **Financial** from the Navigation Pane on the left, and clicking on **General Ledger** in the area page under **Setup | Financial**.

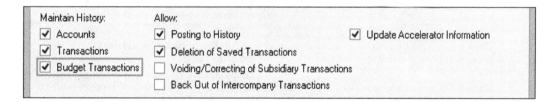

2. Check the **Budget Transactions** checkbox under the **Maintain History** heading.

If you do not mark the **Maintain History** option for **Budget Transactions**, then no record of the budget adjustment is kept when the transaction is posted, which means you cannot see what adjustments have been made to the budget.

To enter a budget transaction, perform the following steps:

1. Open the **Budget Transaction Entry** window in Dynamics GP by clicking on **Financial** from the Navigation Pane on the left, and clicking on **Budget Transactions** in the area page under **Transactions | Financial**.

2. Enter Adjustment to Budget in the **Reference** field.

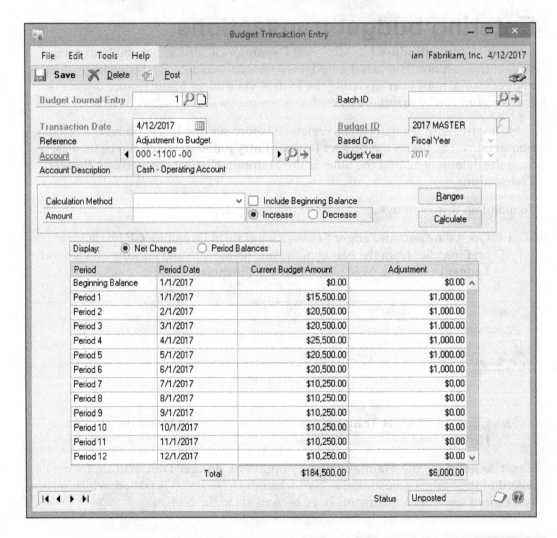

3. Enter 2017 MASTER in the **Budget ID** field.

4. Enter $1,000.00 in the **Adjustment** column for **Period 1** through **Period 6**.

5. Click on **Post** to post the budget transaction and update the budget values.

The budget transaction updates the budget, so that any inquiry or report will show on the budget value plus the budget transaction. Only if the history for the budget transactions is being maintained, will Dynamics GP have any record that a budget transaction has been used.

Summary

In this chapter, we have covered the creation of budgets and their maintenance via both Microsoft Excel and a window in Microsoft Dynamics GP. We followed this up with how to combine budgets and enter budget transactions. In the next chapter, we will take a look at how to report on the budget figures themselves and also in comparison to the actuals.

4
Budget Reporting

In the last chapter, we took a look at creating and maintaining budgets in Dynamics GP. Budgets are of little use unless the information can be inquired or reported upon.

Dynamics GP provides several ways in which this can be accomplished. In this chapter, we will start by taking a look at the inquiries and reports available in Dynamics GP, before moving onto reporting in Dynamics GP and wrapping up with a look at budget reporting using Management Reporter 2012, which is the financial reporting tool for Microsoft Dynamics ERP.

Inquiries

There are a number of standard inquiries available in Dynamics GP, which can be used to inquire upon budget data. As with all inquiries in Dynamics GP, the ones available for budgets inquire upon a single piece of data.

Budget Summary Inquiry

The Budget Summary Inquiry provides a quick and easy-to-use view to see the budget value assigned to an account.

To use the Budget Summary Inquiry, follow the given steps:

1. Open the **Budget Summary Inquiry** window in Dynamics GP by clicking on **Financial** from the Navigation Pane on the left, and clicking on **Budget Summary** in the area page under **Inquiry | Financial**.

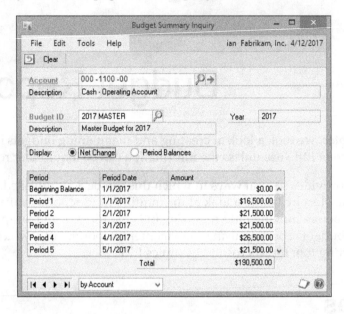

2. Enter 000-1100-00 in the **Account** field to load the account we have used in previous examples.

3. Enter 2017 MASTER in the **Budget ID** field.

4. By default, this inquiry shows the net change of the budget, but can be changed to show the period balances, as shown in the following screenshot, by clicking on the **Period Balances** option under **Display**.

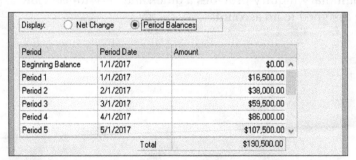

5. Click on **Clear** and then close the window.

The Budget Summary Inquiry is a useful tool to give to budget holders, so they can review the budget values assigned to accounts without giving them access to the budget maintenance where they could make changes.

Budget vs. Actual Inquiry

One of the most useful inquiries that can be made available to budget holders is the Budget vs. Actual Inquiry. It can be used to compare the budgeted values against the transactions that have been entered, while showing the variance as both a functional currency value and percentage.

To use the Budget vs. Actual Inquiry, follow the given steps:

1. Open the **Budget vs. Actual Inquiry** window in Dynamics GP by clicking on **Financial** from the Navigation Pane on the left, and clicking on **Budget vs. Actual** in the area page under **Inquiry | Financial**.

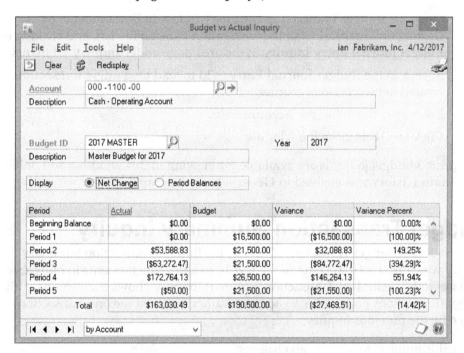

2. Enter 000-1100-00 in the **Account** field.
3. Enter 2017 MASTER in the **Budget ID** field.
4. Click on **Clear** and then close the window.

As with the Budget Summary Inquiry, the Budget vs. Actual Inquiry can be used to display the net change or period balances' figures for the selected account.

Budget Journal Entry Inquiry

As discussed in the previous chapter, budget transactions were introduced in Dynamics GP 2010. Their introduction was accompanied by the Budget Journal Entry Inquiry which allows posted budget journals to be viewed.

This provides the ability to see which budgets have been adjusted and is the reason why using budget transactions to make adjustments is better than just editing the budget in Excel.

To view a posted budget transaction, follow the given steps:

1. Open the **Budget Transaction Inquiry** window in Dynamics GP by clicking on **Financial** from the Navigation Pane on the left, and clicking on **Budget Journal Entry Inquiry** in the area page under **Inquiry | Financials**.

2. Enter 1 in the **Budget Journal Entry** field to load the budget transaction created in the previous chapter.

3. Enter 00-1100-00 in the **Account** field.

4. Click on **OK** to close the window.

Only posted budget journals are available for viewing in this window, and only if **Maintain History** was enabled in **General Ledger Setup**.

Budget Transaction Summary Inquiry

Along with the Budget Transaction Inquiry, the Budget Transaction Summary Inquiry was introduced to Dynamics GP 2010 to allow amendments to budgets to be viewed. The Budget Transaction Summary Inquiry shows a summary of all budget transactions entered for an account, rather than just the one transaction shown by the previous inquiry.

To use this inquiry, follow the given steps:

1. Open the **Budget Transaction Summary Inquiry** window in Dynamics GP by clicking on **Financial** from the Navigation Pane on the left, and clicking on **Budget Transaction Summary** in the area page under **Inquiry | Financial**.

2. Enter 000-1100-00 in the **Account** field.

3. Enter 2017 MASTER in the **Budget ID** field.

Account Rollup Inquiry

Account rollups are inquiries built to allow users to see different GP accounts and their budgets rolled up together, and to provide drill back capability to the details. Additionally, these queries can include calculations for things such as budget versus actual comparisons and calculations.

To an extent, Account Rollup Inquiries function as "Management Reporter Lite", in the way they allow users to access the same functionality of reporting on actual and budget figures for accounts in periods and drill down to see the same details. Account rollups are quicker to use as the more restricted functionality makes them less complicated.

To create an Account Rollup Inquiry for the 2017 SALES budget, follow the given steps:

1. Open the **Account Rollup Inquiry** window in Dynamics GP by clicking on **Financial** from the Navigation Pane on the left, and clicking on **Account Rollup** in the area page under **Inquiry | Financial**.

2. Enter BUDGET-SALES in the **Option ID** field.

3. Tab out of **Option ID** and click on **Yes** on the **Do you want to add this account rollup inquiry option?** question.

4. Set **Sort By** to **Department** and change the number of columns to **3**.

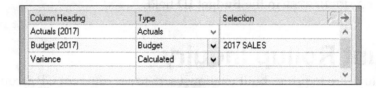

5. In the scrolling window, follow the given steps:

    1. Change the first row's **Column Heading** to `Actuals (2017)`.

    2. Change the second row's **Column Heading** to `Budget (2017)`, set the **Type** to **Budget**, and enter `2017 SALES` into the **Selection** column.

    3. In the third row, enter `Variance` in the **Column heading** field, change the **Type** to **Calculated**, and click on the blue expansion arrow next to the **Selection** heading to open the **Account Rollup Inquiry Calculated Column** window.

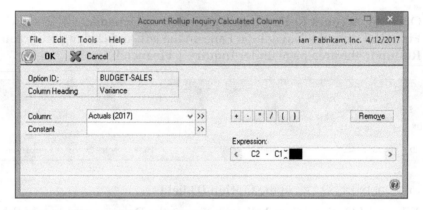

6. In the **Column:** field, click on **Budget (2017)**.

7. Click on the **>>** button to insert `C2` into the **Expression** field.

8. Click on the **–** button to insert a minus sign into the **Expression** field.

9. Change **Column:** to **Actuals (2017)** and click on the **>>** button to insert `C1` into the **Expression** field.

10. Click on **OK** to accept the calculation and close the **Account Rollup Inquiry Calculated Column** window.

11. Enter 300 (the code used for Sales in the chart of accounts) in the **From:** and **To:** fields.

12. Click on **Insert>>** to insert the **Restriction**.

13. Click on **Save** to save the new account rollup option.

14. Click on **Inquiry** to run the **BUDGET-SALES** Account Rollup Inquiry.

15. Click on **Redisplay** to populate the scrolling window with the data for Division 300.

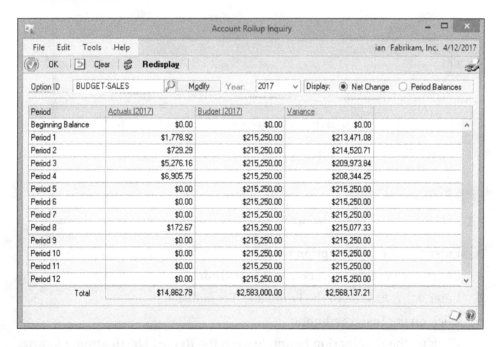

The column headings on the **Account Rollup Inquiry** are hyperlinks, which will open the **Account Rollup Detail Inquiry Zoom** window and which in turn allows you to drill down to either account maintenance or the detail inquiry.

Detailed budget report

Dynamics GP contains only one standard report for budgets, which is a detailed budget report that shows the budget accounts and period amounts.

To generate the report, perform the following steps:

1. Open the **Budget Report** window in Dynamics GP by clicking on **Financial** from the Navigation Pane on the left, and clicking on **Budget** in the area page under **Reports | Financial**.

2. Click on **New** to open the **Budget Report Options** window.

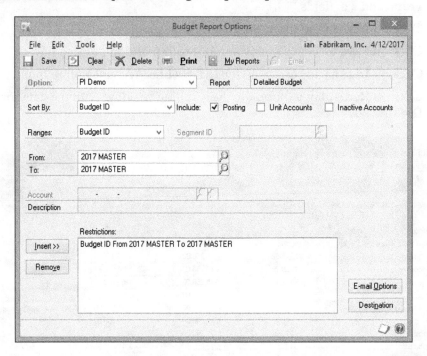

3. Enter BUDGET in the **Option** field.
4. Check the **Posting** checkbox next to **Include:**.
5. Enter 2017 MASTER in the **From:** and **To:** fields.
6. Click on the **Insert>>** button.
7. Click on the **Destination** button to open the **Report Destination** window.
8. Uncheck **Print** and check **Screen**.
9. Click on **OK** to close the **Report Destination** window.

10. Click on **Print**.

```
System:      5/12/2013   10:19:12                    Fabrikam, Inc.                           Page:     1
User Date:   4/12/2017                               BUDGET LIST                              User ID: ian
                                                     General Ledger


Ranges:          From:                         To:
  Budget ID      2017 MASTER                   2017 MASTER
  Description    First                         Last
  Account        First                         Last

Sorted By:  Budget ID/Account
Include:    Posting

^ Inactive Account

Budget ID          Description
-----------------------------------------------------------------------------------------------------------
  Account                      Description                             Account Type
-----------------------------------------------------------------------------------------------------------
2017 MASTER        Master Budget for 2017                                      From:  1/1/2017    To: 12/31/2017
  000-1100-00                  Cash - Operating Account               Posting Account
         Budget Figures:
                         Beginning Balance             $0.00
                         Period 1                 $16,500.00
                         Period 2                 $21,500.00
                         Period 3                 $21,500.00
                         Period 4                 $26,500.00
                         Period 5                 $21,500.00
                         Period 6                 $21,500.00
                         Period 7                 $10,250.00
                         Period 8                 $10,250.00
                         Period 9                 $10,250.00
                         Period 10                $10,250.00
                         Period 11                $10,250.00
                         Period 12                $10,250.00
                                                 ------------------------
                         Budget Total:           $190,500.00
                                                 ========================
```

11. Close **Screen Output – Detailed Budget**.

12. Click on **Save** and close the **Budget Report Options** window.

13. Close the **Budget Report** window.

Budgets in Management Reporter 2012

The inquiries and report in Dynamics GP for budgets are good but fairly limited in functionality. Fortunately, another range of Dynamics products is available for use to report on budgets.

This is the Management Reporter 2012 financial reporting product. With the Dynamics GP 2013 Starter Pack (the base licensing pack), an unlimited number of administrator, designer, generator, and viewer licenses are available.

Management Reporter allows for the reporting of multiple budgets for periods, ranges of periods, or YTD. In this section, we'll take a look at producing a fairly simple budget for the Sales division using the 2017 SALES budget created earlier.

Before producing the report, you will need a fully implemented installation of the latest version of Management Reporter 2012 (at time of writing, this is Rollup 6). You also need security access to Management Reporter and a basic understanding of the reporting product.

We are going to cover a fairly simple report in this section in three parts showing how to create the row definition, column definition, and then the report definition, which pulls the first two together into a working report.

Creating the row definition

To create the row definition, follow the given steps:

1. Launch **Management Reporter 2012** and log into the Fabrikam, Inc. company as normal.

2. Press *Ctrl + Shift + R* to create a new row definition.

3. Click on the **Edit** menu and then click on **Insert Rows from Dimensions**.

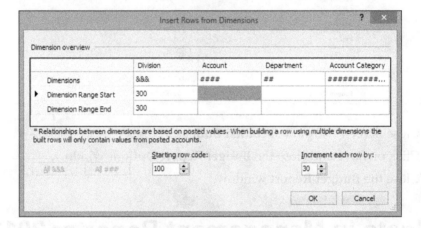

4. In the **Division** column, perform the following steps:

    1. Enter &&& into the **Dimensions** row.

    2. Enter 300 into the **Dimension Range Start** and **Dimension Range End** rows.

5. In the **Account** column, change the value in **Dimensions** to ####.

6. Click on **OK** to close the **Insert Rows from Dimensions** window and update the row definition.

A Row Code	B Description	C Format Code	D Related Formulas / Rows / Units	E Format Override	F Normal Balance	G Print Control	H Column Restriction	I Row Modifier	J Link to Financial Dimensions
100	Sales								+Division = [300]

7. Click on **Save**.

8. Enter BUDGET-SALES in the **Name** field.

9. Enter Budget - Sales in the **Description** field.

10. Click on **OK** and close the row definition.

This row definition is very simple in structure, and will give an overview of the figures for the Sales division. However, with the options on the report definition that we will set later, we'll be able to drill down and see more details.

Creating the column definition

To create the column definition, follow the given steps:

1. Launch **Management Reporter 2012** and log into the Fabrikam, Inc. company.

2. Press *Ctrl + Shift + C* to create a new column definition.

	A	B	C	D	E	F	G
Header 1		Sales Budg…					
Header 2		1 to 3	4 to 6	7 to 9	10 to 12	Year-to-Date	@FiscalYear
Header 3							
Column Type	DESC	FD	FD	FD	FD	FD	FD
Book Code / Attribute Category		2017 SALES	2017 SALES	2017 SALES	2017 SALES	2017 SALES	2017 SALES
Fiscal Year		2017	2017	2017	2017	2017	2017
Period		1:3	4:6	7:9	10:12	BASE	1:12
Periods Covered		PERIODIC	PERIODIC	PERIODIC	PERIODIC	YTD	PERIODIC
Formula							
Column Width	30	14	14	14	14	14	14
Extra Spaces Before Column							
Format / Currency Override							
Print Control		P<=B	P<=B	P<=B	P<=B		

3. Enter Desc in the **Column Type** in column **A**.

4. In column **B**, perform the following steps:

   1. Double-click on the **Header 1** cell and enter Sales Budget @ FiscalYear in the **Column header text** and enter B in **Spread from** and G in **Spread to**.

   2. Click on **Ok** to close the **Column Header** window.

   3. In **Header 2** enter 1 to 3, which is the period range that the column will contain.

4. Enter FD in the **Column Type** row which defines this column as containing either actual or budget figures from the financial dimension.

5. Enter 2017 Sales in the **Book Code / Attribute Category** row to select the required budget.

6. Enter 2017 in the **Fiscal Year** row.

7. Enter 1:3 in the **Period** row, which will calculate the figures for periods 1, 2, and 3.

8. Enter PERIODIC in the **Periods Covered** row.

9. Enter P<=B in the **Print Column** row.

5. Repeat step 4.2 to step 4.8 for 4 to 6, 7 to 9, and 10 to 12 in **Header 2**; 4:6, 7:9, and 10:12 in the **Period** row.

6. In column **F**, perform the following steps:

    1. In **Header 2**, enter Year-to-Date.

    2. Enter FD in the **Column Type** row.

    3. Enter 2017 Sales in the **Book Code / Attribute Category** row.

    4. Enter 2017 in the **Fiscal Year** row.

    5. Enter BASE in the **Period** row.

    6. Enter YTD in the **Periods Covered** row.

7. In column **G**, perform the following steps:

    1. In **Header 2** enter @FiscalYear.

    2. Enter FD in the **Column Type** row.

    3. Enter 2017 Sales in the **Book Code / Attribute Category** row.

    4. Enter 2017 in the **Fiscal Year** row.

    5. Enter 1:12 in the **Period** row.

    6. Enter PERIODIC in the **Periods Covered** row.

8. Click on **Save** to save the new column definition.

9. Enter BUDGET-SALES-2017 in the **Name** field.

10. Enter Budget - Sales 2017 in the **Description** field.

11. Click on **OK** and close the column definition.

Creating the report definition

To create the default records needed for analytical accounting, follow the given steps:

1. Launch **Management Reporter 2012** and log into the Fabrikam, Inc. company as `normal`.

2. Press *Ctrl + Shift + P* to create a new report definition.

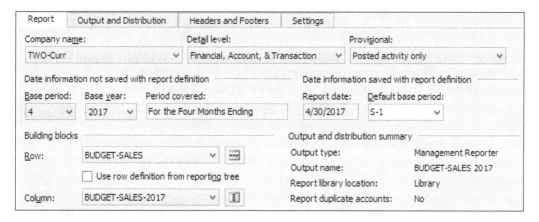

3. Set the **Detail level:** to `Financial, Account, & Transaction`.

4. Fabrikam, Inc. is operating in 2017, so change the **Base Year:** to `2017`.

5. Set the **Row:** to `BUDGET-SALES`.

6. Set the **Column:** to `BUDGET-SALES 2017`.

7. Click on the **Output** and **Distribution** tab.

8. Enter `BUDGET-SALES 2017` in the **Output name:** field.

9. Click on **Save** to save the new column definition.

10. Enter `BUDGET-SALES-2017` in the **Name** field.

11. Enter `Budget - Sales 2017` in the **Description** field.

12. Click on **OK** and close the column definition.

13. Click on **Generate** to produce the report and launch the **Report Viewer**.

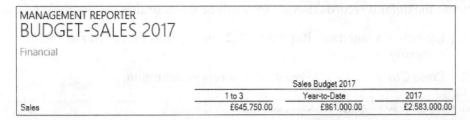

MANAGEMENT REPORTER
BUDGET-SALES 2017
Financial

	Sales Budget 2017		
	1 to 3	Year-to-Date	2017
Sales	£645,750.00	£861,000.00	£2,583,000.00

As the base period was set to April, the print control means only the first of the periodic columns displays on the report. Clicking on the line will drill down to the account level showing the breakdown of the budget values on the accounts.

MANAGEMENT REPORTER
BUDGET-SALES 2017
Financial Account
Sales

	Sales Budget 2017		
	1 to 3	Year-to-Date	2017
Sales:			
300-5100-00- Salaries and Wages - Sales	30,750.00	41,000.00	123,000.00
300-5110-00- Overtime Pay - Sales	30,750.00	41,000.00	123,000.00
300-5120-00- Bonuses - Sales	30,750.00	41,000.00	123,000.00
300-5130-00- Commissions - Sales	30,750.00	41,000.00	123,000.00
300-5140-00- Profit Sharing - Sales	30,750.00	41,000.00	123,000.00
300-5150-00- Employee Benefits - Sales	30,750.00	41,000.00	123,000.00
300-5160-00- Health Insurance Expense - Sales	30,750.00	41,000.00	123,000.00
300-5170-00- Payroll Taxes - Sales	30,750.00	41,000.00	123,000.00
300-6100-00- Training - Sales	30,750.00	41,000.00	123,000.00
300-6120-00- Supplies/Rental - Sales	30,750.00	41,000.00	123,000.00
300-6130-00- Supplies/Hardware - Sales	30,750.00	41,000.00	123,000.00
300-6140-00- Supplies/Software - Sales	30,750.00	41,000.00	123,000.00
300-6150-00- Supplies-Allocated - Sales	30,750.00	41,000.00	123,000.00
300-6160-00- Dues & Subscriptions - Sales	30,750.00	41,000.00	123,000.00
300-6170-00- Repairs & Maintenance - Sales	30,750.00	41,000.00	123,000.00
300-6180-00- Rent Expense - Sales	30,750.00	41,000.00	123,000.00
300-6190-00- Utilities Expense - Sales	30,750.00	41,000.00	123,000.00
300-6500-00- Postage/Freight - Sales	30,750.00	41,000.00	123,000.00
300-6510-00- Telephone - Sales	30,750.00	41,000.00	123,000.00
300-6520-00- Travel - Sales	30,750.00	41,000.00	123,000.00
300-6530-00- Meals/Entertainment - Sales	30,750.00	41,000.00	123,000.00
Total Sales	645,750.00	861,000.00	2,583,000.00

As with report created in Management Reporter, additional columns can be added to the column definition to include actual figures in the report as well as calculation fields.

Summary

In this chapter, we have taken a look at the inquiries and reports available within a standard implementation of Microsoft Dynamics GP as well as looking at how Management Reporter 2012 can be used to extend this reporting.

In the next chapter, we will take a look at how Purchase Order Commitments can be used to control expenditure.

5
Purchase Order Commitments

Purchase Order Commitments (PO Commitments) are available in Microsoft Dynamics GP as a part of the Purchase Order Enhancements module, which also includes PO Approvals within Purchase Order Processing.

A Purchase Order Commitment is a way to reserve funds when a PO is entered in the system to ensure that the funds remain available when the goods are received and invoiced. PO Commitments works by comparing the committed PO amounts along with the actual values for the received POs compared to the budget values for the period.

In this chapter we'll take a look at enabling PO Commitments, entering transactions, and then reporting on the commitments. By following these steps, you will learn how to use PO Commitments in Dynamics GP to gain control over purchasing.

Enabling PO Commitments

Before Purchase Order Commitments can be used, the function in Purchase Order Enhancements needs to be enabled.

To enable Purchase Order Commitments, follow these steps:

1. Open the **PO Enhancements Setup** window in Dynamics GP by selecting **Financial** from the Navigation Pane on the left, and then clicking on **Purchase Order Enhancements** in the area page under **Setup**.

2. Mark the **Activate Commitments** checkbox.

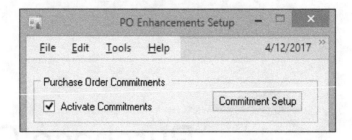

3. Click the **Commitment Setup** button to open the **PO Commitments Setup** window.

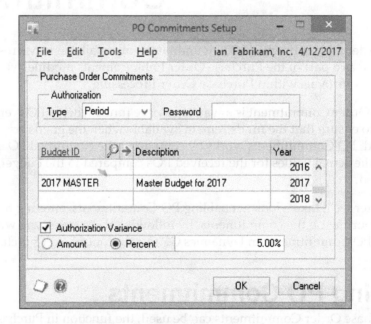

4. Change the **Authorization Type** to **Period**.

5. In the scrolling window, scroll down to **2017** and enter 2017 MASTER into the **Budget ID** field.

6. Mark the **Authorization Variance** checkbox to enable variances.

7. Click on the **Percent** option and enter 5.00% in the next field.

8. Click on **OK** to accept the changes.

9. Click on **OK** on the **Changes have been made to PO Commitments Setup. Any active users must log in again to inherit these changes.** message.

10. Click on **OK** on the **A fiscal year or period within a fiscal year isn't assigned a budget. Purchase amounts entered in this year or period will not be committed.** message.

11. Click on **OK** to accept the changes, and close the **PO Enhancements Setup** window.

12. Click on **No** in response to the message **One or more purchase orders have not been committed. Do you wish to generate a report?**.

> With Purchase Order Commitments now enabled, any fiscal year with a commitment budget defined will be compared to the budget and committed amounts to see if a purchase order can be entered.
>
> For every year that commitments are to be used, a budget is required. In this example, I have used the 2017 MASTER budget, but there is no requirement to use the Master budget.

Entering a Purchase Order Commitment

Now that we have enabled PO Commitments and selected the budget to use for the commitments, it is time to enter a transaction.

This example will show a standard PO for a narrative item being entered, which exceeds the budget value.

To enter a Purchase Order Commitment, perform the following steps:

1. Open the **Purchase Order Entry** window in Dynamics GP by selecting **Purchasing** from the Navigation Pane on the left, and then clicking on **Assignment** in the area page under **Transactions**.

2. Set **Standard** in the **Type:** field, and tab through the **PO Number** field to have one assigned.

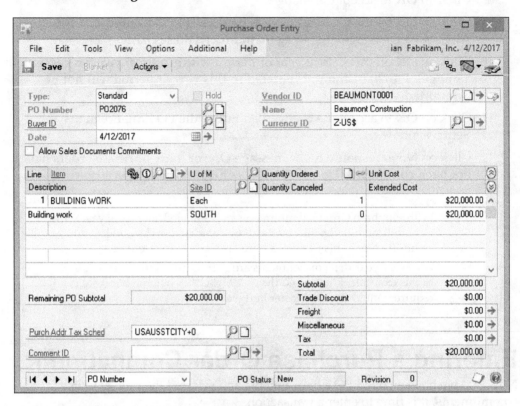

3. Enter BEAUMONT0001 in the **Vendor ID** field.
4. Enter BUILDING WORK in the **Item** field.
5. Tab through and enter Each in the **U of M** field.
6. Enter a quantity of 1 in the **Quantity Ordered** field.

7. Enter $20,000.00 in the **Unit Cost** field.

8. Enter Building work in the **Description** field.

9. Enter SOUTH in the **Site ID** field.

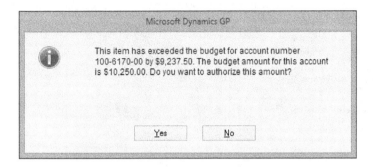

10. A question dialog will be displayed, if the amount being entered is for more than the budget for the selected account, so click on **Yes** to accept the commitment. If a password had been entered on the **PO Commitments Setup** window, the prompt would have requested the password be entered rather than just clicking on **Yes**.

11. Click on **Save**, and close the **Purchase Order Entry** window.

As you can see, enabling PO Commitments only adds one extra step to entering a purchase order, and this extra step only occurs if the budget against the commitment budget is exceeded.

Budget vs Actual & Committed Inquiry

Dynamics GP does not include many inquiries and has no reports for reporting on PO Commitments. The one inquiry it does have is actually quite a useful one. The **Budget vs Actual & Committed Inquiry** allows committed (unreceived POs) and actual (received POs) to be compared against budget values.

To use the **Budget vs Actual & Committed** inquiry, perform the following steps:

1. Open the **Budget vs Actual & Committed Inquiry** window in Dynamics GP by selecting **Budget vs Actual & Committed** from the Navigation Pane on the left, and then clicking on **Assignment** in the area page under **Inquiry**.

2. Enter 100-6170-00 in the **Account** field.

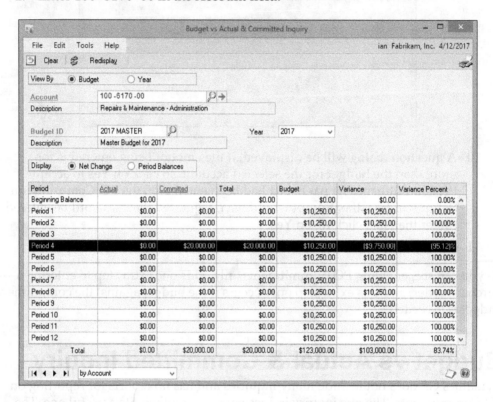

3. The Master 2017 budget will default into the **Budget ID** field.

4. After selecting a period, clicking on the **Actual** column heading will launch the standard **Detail Inquiry** window. Click on the **Committed** heading to launch the **Committed Detail Inquiry** window, which shows details of the transaction and allows you to drill down to the **Purchase Order Entry Zoom** window.

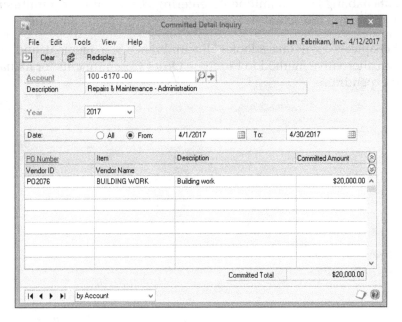

When a PO is received, the committed value is removed and added to actuals, but the total does not change as the posted transaction is still counted against the budget. This means that a PO exceeding the commitment budget will still receive the warning message as the system compares against the total value of committed and actuals.

Summary

The purpose of PO Commitments is to allow an organization to control spending by preventing POs being raised, which exceed the specified budget. In this chapter we looked at enabling PO Commitments, entering POs to raise a commitment, and then how to report on the actual and committed versus budget amounts.

In the next chapter we will take a look at Encumbrance Management, and how it can be used as an alternative method to Purchase Order Commitments for managing and controlling expenditure.

6
Encumbrance Management

Encumbrance Management enables funds to be reserved from a budget when a purchase order is created. The creation of encumbrances reduces the risk of overspending and ensures that funds will be available when payments become due. This module is often used by non-profit organizations as a part of their budget and fund accounting.

Encumbrances and PO Commitments are very similar in form and function, but there are differences in how Dynamics GP handles them. The basic differences are:

- Encumbrance Management tracks history in Dynamics GP, whereas PO Commitments does not

- Encumbrance Management requires each open year to have a budget selected for encumbering transactions, whereas PO Commitments allow individual years to have a budget defined against them

- Encumbrance Management does not integrate with Business Portal Requisition Management, but PO Commitments does

In this chapter we will take a look at the setup of Encumbrance Management, entering purchase orders, and then reporting and enquiring on the encumbrances.

Setting up Encumbrance Management

When Encumbrance Management is being configured, it is recommended that all other users log out of Dynamics GP.

To set up Encumbrance Management, perform the following steps:

1. Open the **Encumbrance Setup** window in Dynamics GP by selecting **Purchasing** from the Navigation Pane on the left, and then clicking on **Encumbrance Management** in the area page under **Setup**.

2. Mark the **Enable Encumbrance Management** checkbox.

3. Leave **Budget Type** set to **General Ledger Budgets**. Encumbrance Management also allows encumbrances against Analytical Accounting and Grant Management budgets, but in this book we will focus on using the standard General Ledger budgets that we looked at in *Chapter 3, Budget Creation and Maintenance.*

4. Set the **Tracking Method** to **Period** so that the purchase order line amounts are compared to the budget and actual amounts for the period. The other options available for **Tracking Method** are:

   ° **Fiscal Year**, where the purchase line amount is compared to the total budget and actual for the fiscal year. This tracking method is not the one I would recommend, as it would allow a transaction in the first fiscal period to use the entire year's budget.

   ° **Budget-to-Date** is one, along with **Period**, which I tend to recommend. This method allows any unused period's budget amount to be used in the current period.

   ° **Total Budget** allows for tracking amounts against a budget, which does not align with a fiscal year. This method is also recommended for use when blanket purchase orders are being used.

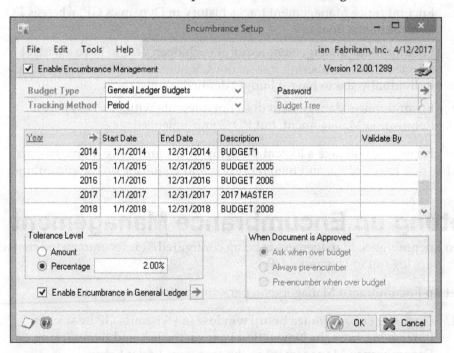

5. Click on the expansion button (blue arrow) in the **Year** scrolling window to open the **Encumbrance Budget Setup** window.

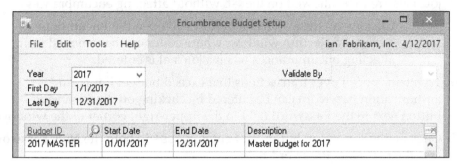

6. In the **Year** drop-down selector, enter or do a lookup, and select the relevant budget (the **Description** can be changed if desired).

   As of Dynamics GP 2013, Encumbrance Management allows multiple budgets to be selected for each fiscal year; to select more than one budget, enter each one on a different line in the scrolling window; this is useful when departments are using separate budgets.

7. When all years have been assigned to use at least one budget, click on the **OK** button to close the **Encumbrance Budget Setup** window.

8. Under **Tolerance Level**, click on **Percentage** and enter 2.00% to allow a variance between the actual and budget amounts for the period.

   The following table describes how positive and negative amounts work with each tolerance type level:

	If you enter a positive value	If you enter a negative value
Amount	Purchases can exceed the budget amount by the currency amount you specify	Purchases must be under the budget amount by the currency amount you specify
Percentage	Purchases can exceed the budget amount by the percentage you specify	Purchases must be under the budget amount by the percentage you specify

Source: *Microsoft Dynamics GP Not for Profit Accounting manual © Microsoft Corporation*

9. By default, when setting up Encumbrance Management, **Enable Encumbrance in General Ledger** will be checked; uncheck it if journals are to be allowed on the GL without affecting encumbrances.

   ° Clicking on the expansion button will open the **Encumbrance Account Selection** window, where codes can be removed from affecting encumbrances when a journal is entered.

10. To retain control over transactions that exceed budget limits, an authorization password can be entered by clicking on the expansion button next to the **Password** field in the upper-right corner of the window.

11. Click on the expansion button and enter ACCESS in both the **New Password** and **Reenter New Password** fields.

12. Click on **OK** to close the **Encumbrance Password Setup** window.

13. Click on **OK** to accept the setup and close the **Encumbrance Setup** window.

With Encumbrance Management set up for use, we can move on to entering transactions.

Encumbrance statuses

When Encumbrance Management setup changes are saved, all purchase orders and related receiving transactions are evaluated with an encumbrance; the pre-encumbrance or pre-budget amount will be created using the required by date.

The following table describes the statuses:

Status	Description
Encumbered	The purchase order line item is within the budget you set up (plus the tolerable range, if you've set up budget tolerances). Also, the status is encumbered if the budget has been exceeded, but the purchase has been authorized.
Pre-Encumbered	The purchase order line item is not within the budgeted amount (plus the tolerable range, if you've set up budget tolerances).
Pre-Budget	The purchase order has not been approved. This status allows encumbrance records to be created for the purchase order line item. Budgets aren't affected because the purchase order hasn't been approved. This status is used only if a Workflow or purchase order approvals in Purchase Order Enhancements is being used.
	When the purchase order is approved and is within the budget, the status will change from pre-budget to encumbered or pre-encumbered based on the settings you chose in the **Encumbrance Setup** window.

Status	Description
Invalid	The purchase order line item is missing information or information is not valid.
Limbo	The purchase order line item is not validated against the budget.

Source: *Microsoft Dynamics GP Not for Profit Accounting manual © Microsoft Corporation*

The same encumbrance statuses are applied to amounts on purchase orders as they are entered. If you're using blanket or drop-ship purchase orders, the control line will have a status of **Pre-Encumbered** regardless of the status amount.

Transaction entry

Encumbrances are created automatically when a purchase order is entered using the statuses in the preceding table. An encumbrance is automatically authorized when the transaction amount fits within the budget amount, which is calculated using the following equation:

Budget amount - Actual amount - Encumbrance amount

If the resulting value is a negative amount, the transaction will not be encumbered. As an example, if you have a budget amount of $20,000 and enter a transaction for $12,000, the remaining budget amount is $8,000. Any transaction of more than $8,000 will exceed the budget value and not be automatically encumbered, assuming a tolerance has not been defined in Encumbrance Management Setup.

When the receiving transaction is posted, or a purchase order is deleted or canceled, the encumbrance amount is liquidated (reduced), and in the case of posting, the actual amount is increased by the same value so there is no difference in the remaining budget amount.

Encumbrance Management does not change the process of entering a purchase order. When PO Approvals are being used and a user who does not have approval authority enters a purchase order, the encumbrance needs to be reviewed and authorized; likewise, when a transaction exceeds the budgeted amount, authorization is required.

To authorize purchase orders that are pre-encumbered, or pre-budget when PO Approvals is being used, perform the following steps:

1. Open the **Mass Encumbrance** window in Dynamics GP by selecting **Purchasing** from the Navigation Pane on the left, and then clicking on **Mass Encumbrance** in the area page under **Transactions | Encumbrance Management**.

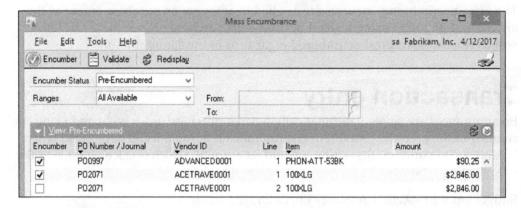

2. If PO Approvals is being used, change **Encumber Status** to **Pre-Budget**, otherwise leave it as the default of **Pre-Encumbered**.
3. Mark the **Encumber** checkbox next to **PO0997** and **PO2071**.
4. Click on the **Encumber** button on the toolbar.
5. If the selected transactions exceed the budgeted values, a confirmation dialog box will be displayed. Click on **Yes** and then enter the password to proceed with the Encumbrance.

Encumbrance inquiries

There are a number of inquiry windows available in Dynamics GP to look at Encumbrance Management.

Encumbrance Summary Inquiry

The **Encumbrance Summary Inquiry** window can be used to view a current or historical summary report of actual and encumbered transactions for a selected budget and a range of accounts. To use the inquiry, perform the following steps:

1. Open the **Encumbrance Summary Inquiry** window in Dynamics GP by selecting **Purchasing** from the Navigation Pane on the left, and then clicking on **Summary** in the area page under **Inquiry**.

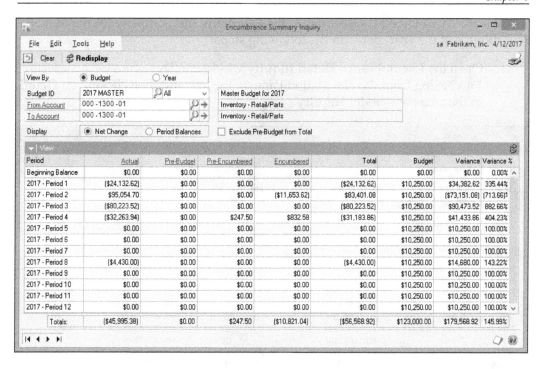

2. The **Budget ID** field will default to the budget selected for the fiscal year the user date is in.

3. Enter 000-1300-01 in both the **From Account** and **To Account** fields.

4. Click on the **Redisplay** button to generate the inquiry.

As is standard with Dynamics GP inquiry windows, the scrolling window has a number of links in the column headings, which load a window for the selected period. Clicking on the **Actual** link will load the **General Ledger Detail Inquiry** window, while clicking on any one among **Pre-Budget**, **Pre-Encumbered**, or **Encumbered** will load the **Encumbrance Detail Inquiry** window.

Encumbrance Detail Inquiry

The **Encumbrance Detail Inquiry** window can be used to see the details of encumbrances for a range of dates and accounts. It can also be used to filter the details by the encumbrance status.

To view the encumbered transactions in the **Fabrikam, Inc.** company for the first four months of the year, perform the following steps:

1. Open the **Encumbrance Detail Inquiry** window in Dynamics GP by selecting **Purchasing** from the Navigation Pane on the left, and then clicking on **Detail** in the area page under **Inquiry**.

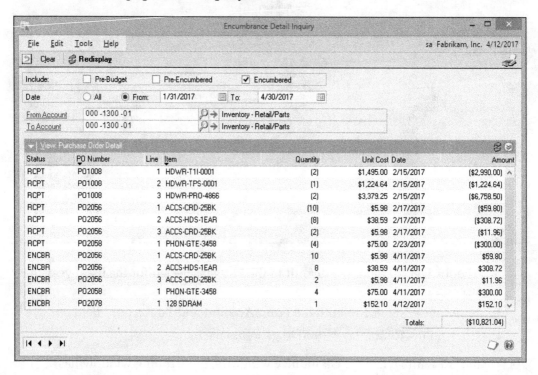

2. Uncheck the **Pre-Encumbered** checkbox to only include encumbered transactions.

3. Click on the **Date From** button and enter 01312017 in the **From** field and 30042017 in the **To** field.

4. Enter 000-1300-01 in both the **From Account** and **To Account** fields.

5. Click on **Redisplay** to refresh the data.

Encumbrance PO Inquiry

The **Encumbrance PO Inquiry** window can be used to view both a summary and detailed view of encumbrances for a selected purchase order.

To use the inquiry, follow these steps:

1. Open the **Encumbrance PO Inquiry** window in Dynamics GP by selecting **Purchasing** from the Navigation Pane on the left, and then clicking on **PO Detail** in the area page under **Transactions | Encumbrance Management**.

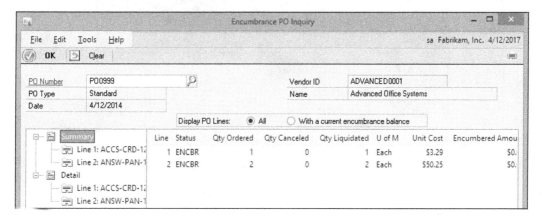

2. Enter PO0999 in the **PO Number** field and press *Tab*.

By default, the inquiry will show the summary information for the encumbrances; clicking on any of the nodes on the tree view will change the detail view to the right. If **Detail** is selected, the view will display the details of the encumbrance, including all status changes.

Encumbrance GL Inquiry

The GL Inquiry functions in the same way as the PO Inquiry by allowing the encumbrance status for each line of a general journal.

Encumbrance Reports

In addition to the inquiries there are also some reports available for year-end reporting. To produce these reports, perform the following steps:

1. Open the **Encumbrance Print Options** window in Dynamics GP by selecting **Purchasing** from the Navigation Pane on the left, and then clicking on **Year End Encumbrance Management Reports** in the area page under **Reports**.

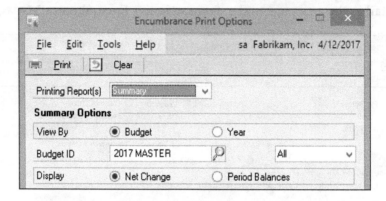

2. The **Budget ID** for the budget the user date falls into will display by default. Click on **Print** to print the summary report.

3. If a detailed report is required, change **Printing Report(s)** to **Detail**.

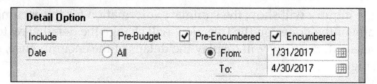

4. Enter 01312017 in the **Date From** field, and 04302017 in the **Date To** field.

5. Click on **Print** to print the detailed report.

There is also an option to print both the reports at the same time by changing **Printing Report(s)** to **Summary And Detail**.

Year-end processes

The **Year End Encumbrance Transfer** window can be used to transfer encumbrances from the previous year to the current one. The transfer process will automatically liquidate encumbered amounts in the previous year and update open purchase orders, which will be delivered in the current year. During the transfer, you can also decrease budget amounts for the previous fiscal year and increase the corresponding budget amounts for the current one.

To perform a year-end encumbrance transfer, perform the following steps:

1. Open the **Year End Encumbrance Transfer** window in Dynamics GP by selecting **Purchasing** from the Navigation Pane on the left, and then clicking on **Year End Encumbrance Transfer** in the area page under **Routines**.

2. Enter 2014 in the **Year** field and press *Tab*.
3. If desired, mark the **Include corresponding budget amounts** checkbox, and then click on **Transfer** to perform the year-end process.

The **Decrease budget amounts for previous fiscal year** checkbox is only enabled when the selected budget has an end date after the end of the fiscal year.

Summary

In this chapter we have introduced the Encumbrance Management module of Dynamics GP, which allows funds to be reserved when a purchase order is entered, thereby reducing the risk of overspending by ensuring that the funds are available when payment becomes due.

As we have discussed at the start of the chapter, Encumbrance Management and PO Commitments are very similar, so a review of requirements should be conducted before one of them is enabled to ensure the required functionality is available to users.

Index

C

Cash Flow Calendar
about 35
launching, from Cash Flow Explorer 38
viewing, steps 35, 36
Cash Flow Explorer
Cash Flow Calendar, launching from 38
using, steps 36, 37
cash flow forecast
creating 33, 34
viewing 37
Cash Flow Management
about 33
tasks 33

D

default records
creating, for Analytical Accounting 5, 6
detailed budget report
about 62
generating 62, 63
Distribution Query Wizard
about 27
using 27-29
duplicate analysis information 19
Dynamics GP
budget, creating 43

E

Encumbrance Detail Inquiry 85, 86
Encumbrance GL Inquiry 87
Encumbrance inquiries
about 84
Encumbrance Detail Inquiry 85, 86
Encumbrance GL Inquiry 87
Encumbrance PO Inquiry 87
Encumbrance Summary Inquiry 84, 85
Encumbrance Management
about 79
setting up, steps 79-82
transaction entry 83, 84
versus PO Commitments 79
Encumbrance PO Inquiry 87

Encumbrance Reports
about 88
producing, steps 88
Encumbrance statuses
about 82
Encumbered 82
Invalid 83
Limbo 83
Pre-budget 82
Pre-Encumbered 82
Encumbrance Summary Inquiry
using, steps 84, 85

F

Fixed Asset Management
Analytical Accounting, integrating with 19

I

inquiries, Dynamics GP
about 55
Budget Journal Entry Inquiry 58
Budget Summary Inquiry 55-57
Budget Transaction Summary Inquiry 58
Budget vs. Actual Inquiry 57
inquries, Analytical Accounting
Analytical Accounting Budget vs
  Actual Inquiry 30
Distribution Query Wizard 27-29
Journal Entry Inquiry 26
Multilevel Query Wizard 29, 30
Transaction Dimension Relation 26

J

Journal Entry Inquiry 26

M

Management Reporter 2012
budget reporting 63
Microsoft
used, for amending budget 48
Microsoft Dynamics GP
budget, editing through 49

Microsoft Excel
  budget, creating 44, 45
  budget, editing 46
  budget, importing from 46, 47
  budgets, exporting to 24
Multilevel Query Wizard 29

O

options, Analytical Accounting
  amending 10, 11

P

PO Commitments
  about 71
  enabling, steps 71-73
  entering, steps 73-75
  versus Encumbrance Management 79
posted budget transaction
  viewing, steps 58
posting options
  setting up 6, 7
Purchase Order Commitments. *See* PO
      Commitments

S

security roles
  assigning, to users 8, 9

T

tasks
  assigning 8, 9
transaction
  entering, with Analytical Accounting
      information 17-19
Transaction Dimension Relation 26
transaction dimensions
  types 12
  user access, granting to 16, 17
transaction entry, Encumbrance
      Management 83, 84

U

user access
  granting, to transaction dimensions 16, 17
users
  security role, assigning to 8, 9

W

weekly cash flow reports
  printing 38
what if transaction
  using, steps 39-41

Y

year-end closing
  performing 24
year-end encumbrance transfer
  performing, steps 89

Thank you for buying
Microsoft Dynamics GP 2013
Financial Management

About Packt Publishing

Packt, pronounced 'packed', published its first book "Mastering phpMyAdmin for Effective MySQL Management" in April 2004 and subsequently continued to specialize in publishing highly focused books on specific technologies and solutions.

Our books and publications share the experiences of your fellow IT professionals in adapting and customizing today's systems, applications, and frameworks. Our solution based books give you the knowledge and power to customize the software and technologies you're using to get the job done. Packt books are more specific and less general than the IT books you have seen in the past. Our unique business model allows us to bring you more focused information, giving you more of what you need to know, and less of what you don't.

Packt is a modern, yet unique publishing company, which focuses on producing quality, cutting-edge books for communities of developers, administrators, and newbies alike. For more information, please visit our website: www.packtpub.com.

About Packt Enterprise

In 2010, Packt launched two new brands, Packt Enterprise and Packt Open Source, in order to continue its focus on specialization. This book is part of the Packt Enterprise brand, home to books published on enterprise software – software created by major vendors, including (but not limited to) IBM, Microsoft and Oracle, often for use in other corporations. Its titles will offer information relevant to a range of users of this software, including administrators, developers, architects, and end users.

Writing for Packt

We welcome all inquiries from people who are interested in authoring. Book proposals should be sent to author@packtpub.com. If your book idea is still at an early stage and you would like to discuss it first before writing a formal book proposal, contact us; one of our commissioning editors will get in touch with you.

We're not just looking for published authors; if you have strong technical skills but no writing experience, our experienced editors can help you develop a writing career, or simply get some additional reward for your expertise.

Developing Microsoft Dynamics GP Business Applications

ISBN: 978-1-84968-026-4   Paperback: 590 pages

Build dynamic, mission critical applications with this hands-on guide

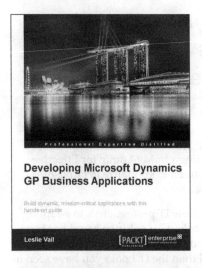

Developing Microsoft Dynamics GP Business Applications

Build dynamic, mission-critical applications with this hands-on guide

Leslie Vail

1. Make your business more efficient with fully customizable applications

2. Develop mission critical applications with Microsoft Dynamics GP

3. Learn how to enhance your application with sanScript

Microsoft Dynamics GP 2013 Cookbook

ISBN: 978-1-84968-938-0   Paperback: 348 pages

Over 110 immediately usable and effective recipes to solve real-world Dynamics GP problems

Microsoft Dynamics GP 2013 Cookbook

Over 110 immediately usable and effective recipes to solve real-word Dynamics GP problems

Ian Grieve   Mark Polino

1. Understand the various tips and tricks to master Dynamics GP, and improve your system's stability in order to enable you to get work done faster

2. Discover how to solve real world problems in Microsoft Dynamics GP 2013 with easy-to-understand and practical recipes

3. Access proven and effective Dynamics GP techniques from authors with vast and rich experience in Dynamics GP

Please check **www.PacktPub.com** for information on our titles

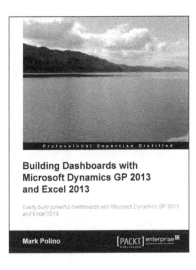

Building Dashboards with Microsoft Dynamics GP 2013 and Excel 2013

ISBN: 978-1-84968-906-9   Paperback: 286 pages

Easily build powerful dashboards with Microsoft Dynamics GP 2013 and Excel

1. Build a dashboard using Excel 2013 with information from Microsoft Dynamics GP 2013

2. Make Excel a true business intelligence tool with charts, sparklines, slicers, and more

3. Utilize PowerPivot's full potential to create even more complex dashboards

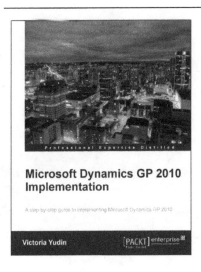

Microsoft Dynamics GP 2010 Implementation

ISBN: 978-1-84968-032-5   Paperback: 376 pages

A step-by-step guide to implementing Microsoft Dynamics GP 2010

1. Master how to implement Microsoft Dynamics GP 2010 with real world examples and guidance from a Microsoft Dynamics GP MVP

2. Understand how to install Microsoft Dynamics GP 2010 and related applications, following detailed, step-by-step instructions

3. Learn how to set-up the core Microsoft Dynamics GP modules effectively

Please check **www.PacktPub.com** for information on our titles